Harvard Studies in Sociology —

Outstanding Dissertations and Monographs

Twenty-two Distinguished Works from the Past Fifty Years

General Editors

Aage Sørensen
Liah Greenfield

Department of Sociology
Harvard University

A GARLAND SERIES

Titles in The Series

Stephen D. Berger
The Development of Legitimating Ideas: Intellectuals and Politicians in Postwar Western Germany.

Ronald Breiger
Explorations in Structural Analysis: Dual and Multiple Networks of Social Interaction.

Gregg Carr
Residence and Social Status: The Development of Seventeenth-Century London.

William K. Cummings
The Changing Academic Marketplace and University Reform in Japan.

Thomas H. Davenport
Virtuous Pagans: Unreligious People in America.

James H. Davis
Living Rooms as Symbols of Status: A Study of Social Judgment.

Erif M. Leifer
Actors as Observers: A Theory of Skill and Social Relationships.

Bonnie Menes Kahn
My Father Spoke French: Nationalism in Alsace, 1871–1914.

Victor Nee
Social Exchange and Political Process in Maoist China.

Nerys Patterson
Cattle Lords and Clansmen: Kinship and Rank in Early Ireland.

Victor Perez-Diaz
Structure and Change in Castilian Peasant Communties.

Lauri Perman
The Other Side of the Coin: The Nonmonetary Characteristics of Jobs.

Michael Schudson
Origins of the Ideal of Objectivity in the Professions: Studies in the History of American Journalism and American Law, 1830–1940.

Rebecca Stafford
The Potent College: The Effect of Organizational Structure Upon Value and Attitude Formation.

Patricia G. Steinhoff
Tenko: Ideology and Societal Integration in Prewar Japan.

F. X. Sutton
Ideology and Social Structure: A Study of Radical Marxism.

Edward A. Tiryakian
The Evaluation of Occupations in a Developing Country: The Philippines.

Ezra F. Vogel
The Marital Relationship of Parents and the Emotionally Disturbed Child.

Robert J. Werlin
The English Novel and the Industrial Revolution: A Study in the Sociology of Literature.

Richard H. Williams
The Expression of Common Value Attitudes Toward Suffering in the Symbolism of Medieval Art.

Robert N. Wilson
The American Poet: A Role Investigation.

The Evaluation of Occupations in a Developing Country
The Philippines

Edward A. Tiryakian

GARLAND PUBLISHING
NEW YORK & LONDON
1990

Library of Congress Cataloging-in-Publication Data

Tiryakian, Edward A.
      The evaluation of occupations in a developing country :
the Philippines / Edward A. Tiryakian.
          p. cm. — (Harvard studies in sociology)
Includes bibliographical references.
ISBN 0-8240-2762-0 (alk. paper)
1. Occupational surveys—Philippines. 2. Philippines—
Occupations. 3. Social classes—Philippines. 4. Philippines—
Economic conditions—1946–1986. I. Title. II. Series.
HD5825.A6T57   1990
331.7'009599—dc20   90-21546

Printed on acid-free, 250-year-life paper
Manufactured in the United States of America

Design by Julie Threlkeld

CONTENTS

PREFACE

THE PHILIPPINES FOUR DECADES LATER:
A SOCIOLOGICAL RETROSPECTIVE

It is both gratifying and challenging to have one's dissertation study published in this distinguished series. The challenge comes in rereading a research conducted at a very early stage in one's professional career and evaluating how it appears in retrospect. I do not intend for this introduction to be an autobiographical odyssey. However, it may be noted at the beginning that even though my professional interests have led me away from the empirical research I carried out in the Philippines, the field experience of gathering data in a "Third World" country has been of lasting value. Sociological research methods, particularly quantitative ones analyzing available data sets, have become much more sophisticated and rigorous in the past four decades. Nonetheless, I regard it as essential for students of sociology (undergraduates and graduates) to also get direct exposure to societal conditions they analyze abstractly.

In this regard, the distinguished contemporary French social scientist Alain Touraine has repeatedly called on sociologists to return centrality to the "actor," to the subject of social action (Touraine 1984). Touraine is informed by his participation in contemporary European social movements and field experience in Latin America. I share his perspective on "a theory of action" as fundamental to sociological analysis, but without field contact, how can sociologists really discuss what "action" means to actors? How can sociologists talk validly about the problems and concerns of collectivities who seek to transform their social environment? By no means did the study I carried out in Central Luzon in the early 1950s qualify me as a specialist or expert on the Philippines, nor in terms of broader analytical considerations, did this study in itself provide answers to important questions of social development. But the study and the background research experiences have provided me with a "stock of knowledge" about the world that continues to fuel my theoretical reflections and comparative analysis on such varied topics as "modernity," "national identity," and "colonial situation."

It was more by chance than by design that I got to the Philippines in the first place. As a graduate student in Social Relations at Harvard I had taken a seminar offered by Talcott Parsons, Samuel Stouffer and Florence Kluckhohn. Florence Kluckhohn, who considered herself a sociologist-anthropologist, advised me to do a dissertation outside the United States. Taking her advice, I applied (with my wife) for a Fulbright research award to study on a comparative basis race relations in South Africa. We were subsequently informed that there would be no Fulbright grants to South Africa but that there were openings for both of us in the Philippines. The topic for research in the Philippines was consequently different from what I had first envisaged but it was related to one of my graduate areas of specialization, namely comparative aspects of industrialization.

There was another sociology student who took the same seminar, received the same advice from Florence Kluckhohn, and eventually did his dissertation in East Asia, rather than Southeast Asia. That person was Ezra Vogel, today one of our most eminent specialists of China and Japan. During the course of our long friendship, I have jocularly discussed with him his good fortune in picking out for his dissertation a country that has shown--with a vengeance, one might even say--how successful a non-Western country can become at development.[1] On the other hand, the country that I studied has not been a pacesetter but rather a laggard. After some false starts at development, its democratic future today appears fragile at best, while its economic growth rate has become mired in a heavy burden of external debt, low rates of investment and rising unemployment.

In the mid-1950s when I went to the Philippines and Ezra Vogel to Japan, it was not obvious which of these two countries of the Far East would have a successful adjustment to the post-war world and which would not. After all, Japan had lost the war and with it its overseas empire; though neither country was self-sufficient in energy needed for industrial development, the Philippines had greater natural resources. Moreover, the Philippines was a showcase for democracy in the Far East, closely allied to the United States which had kept its promise and granted it independence in 1946. The Philippines was pivotal to American defense strategy in the Far East, with formidable military bases at Clark Field for the Air Force and Subic Bay for the Navy. Filipinos were the most pro-American people in that region of the world, and English was the *lingua franca* of the country, reflecting the anglicization of education during the four decades of American administration.

When the Association of Southeast Asian Nations (ASEAN) was formed in 1967 to ward off the threat of Communist take over in that region by strengthening cooperation, it seemed natural for the Philippines to play a major role economically and politically. As Wong noted, the Philippines shared with Indonesia, Malaysia, Singapore and Thailand the desire "to diversify the economy from an over-reliance on primary exports, to promote faster economic growth and to create more employment," but what made the former distinct was that the industrialization experience of the Philippines was the longest in the region (Wong 1979: 67). Yet, observed Wong, the manufacturing sector in the Philippines not only failed to achieve take-off but in fact the Philippines can be used to "highlight the shortcomings of the import-substitution industrialisation strategy" (*Ibid.*: 68). Not only has the Philippines failed to pursue a successful development export strategy like the East Asian "Confucian" countries (Berger and Hsiao 1988; Gereffi and Wyman 1990), it also is lagging behind the development of the other ASEAN countries. So, for example, in the period 1980-85 while the other ASEAN countries had annual GDP growth rates ranging from 3.5 per cent for Indonesia to 10.2 for Singapore, the Philippines experienced a net decrease of 0.5 per cent (World Bank 1987: 204-05; see also Table 1 this essay for various comparisons with pacesetting East Asian countries).[2]

Economic performance is only one face of development, and as I shall discuss below, even during a period of rather favorable aggregate economic development, social development did not blossom in the Philippines. Political development underwent stagnation and regression subsequent to the period of my study of Central Luzon, culminating in the long years of the Marcos authoritarian regime (1965-1985, particularly from 1972 onward when martial law was imposed). The result was that by the mid-1980s the "development" of the Philippines had become more of a tragic case of "maldevelopment" than of what "modernization theory" tacitly proposed would result from Third World countries emulating Western societal models of development and accepting American assistance in realizing these models.[3]

So a question which I offer the reader as a puzzle that opens up a comparative analysis of development is: What went right with Japan and What went wrong with the Philippines? And it is a question which should be of interest not only to social scientists in the abstract but to Americans in particular because of the relation of the United States to the two countries. Japan has become not only one of our largest trading partners but also a formidable presence in world affairs. General McArthur and the magnanimous American occupation which lasted until 1952 certainly succeeded in laying the basis for an industrially strong Japan as an ally of the United States that would be an important buffer against Communist expansion. But paradoxically, the Philippines, where McArthur had been the 1930s and where he left after the Japanese invasion with the famous words "I shall return," received his benign neglect after 1946. Today, the Philippines is both the only Asian nation with a large Christian majority and a country where Communist insurgency has been expanding its sphere of control.

It is precisely because the situation of the Philippines today at the start of a new decade is in some crucial respects so similar to that of the 1950s when I conducted this study that this needs to be mentioned in a retrospective overview. In 1953-54 when I conducted the field research in Luzon, Ramon Magsaysay was president and immensely popular with nearly all strata of the Filipinos who saw him as a charismatic leader wanting to transform the country into an economically viable democratic society that would provide improved conditions for the common man. When Corazon Aquino assumed office in February 1986 following the bloodless Revolution that toppled Ferdinand Marcos, she received immense popular support in the expectation that she might be able to perform the "Filipino miracle" that had been aborted by the tragic death of Magsaysay while in office. Magsaysay in the 1950s had two powerful enemies: the Hukbalahap movement which had long roots in agrarian unrest in Central Luzon (Kerkvliet 1977) and the ruling elites of the Philippines, well entrenched in party politics and resistant to the attempted land reforms of Magasaysay. Today, Aquino faces similar opposition. Instead of the defunct Huks, the Communist Party with its New People's Army was estimated to control or influence one fifth of the population in the Philippines two years after Aquino's accession, and just 20 years after its formation in 1968 (Kessler 1989: 28, 56). In face of elite opposition, her program of land reform has remained dormant, and a series of attempted military coups have compounded her problems of redressing the economy and attracting foreign investments.

If other countries in Southeast and East Asia, designated at the time with other Third World countries as "underdeveloped,"[4] have been able to put their acts together in the interim since this study was conducted, why not the Philippines? In this region the Philippines should have been a textbook demonstration of "modernization theory" showing that Western stimuli (such as political and educational institutions), market-oriented economic transformations, and a collective desire for "nation-building" can succeed in improving dramatically the standard of living and the quality of life of a society's population. In fact, while the region has witnessed the mushrooming of Newly Industrialized Countries (NICs), which in the past two decades have been the successes of the global economy, the Philippines is more the exception to the rule. It is more in the same company with much of Latin America and Africa. Where lies the fault of the Philippines in not emerging out of the area of social, economic and political morass? Is it due to endogenous or exogenous factors or a combination of both?

These considerations revolve around the general theme of "development" and its problematics. It may seem odd to the reader that I make much of this here while little of this preoccupation appears directly in the study itself. To an important extent this reflects that at the time the study was completed, few sociologists were drawn into the discussions of "development economics," as may be gleaned from the bibliography of the impressive recent review essay by Evans and Stephens (1988). One of the few comparative sociologists at the time was Wilbert E. Moore who opened up sociological overseas research with his *Industrialization and Labor*, subtitled "Social Aspects of Economic Development" (1951). At the very beginning of this book Moore stated "Industrial development, in fact, has become the most commonly prescribed panacea for most of the material woes of mankind and for some less tangible shortcomings as well" (1951: 3), and shortly later he took as a critical sociological query "what are the cultural, institutional, sociopsychological factors that induce or impede the transition from nonindustrial to industrial employment?" (*Ibid.*:5). I cite Moore as representative of the widely shared perspective at the time, undoubtedly naive in retrospective, that the way to bridge the great gap between Western and non-Western countries was through industrialization. What sociology could do in this great task was to point out in so many words the non-rational elements that were roadblocks to a rational industrial social order. Tacitly this rational industrial order, if institutionalized, was seen as having its own internal logic that would impose itself and lead to a convergence of values among modern nations (or at least, between national elites). Thus would be provided the structural basis for an interdependent, stable world, one that would perforce lead to the "end of ideology."

This rather optimistic and uncritical perspective on development did not survive much beyond the 1950s and the Kennedy era. It is beside the point to trace out the acrimonious debates of the 1960s and 1970s, much of which originated in Third World countries such as Africa and Latin America by Marxists and nationalists who saw "development" as a fraudulent endeavor of Western industrial countries to perpetuate economically their domination of the rest of the world. Even aside from these critics, theories of development became castigated by a leading conservative sociologist (Nisbet 1970) and ultimately even economists themselves, such as Hirschman and Streeten, the latter being quoted as saying, "At the end of the day... we must confess that we do not know what causes development and therefore lack a clear agenda for research," (cited in Broad 1988: 234).

Let me broaden these remarks about development by returning to the intellectual and social context of the study, and providing the reader with a brief update on each aspect.

THE INTELLECTUAL CONTEXT OF THE STUDY

The study which I conducted in the Philippines, as the reader will note, was the first to seek comparable data on occupational prestige with those that had been gathered in various industrial settings. The Philippines was something of a "traditional" society in terms of a high proportion of the labor force being employed in "traditional," pre-industrial sectors. However, it also had a "modern" emphasis in terms of the educational structure that received high priority early on in the American administration.

Moreover, once I got to Luzon I became aware of an American cultural presence that coexisted with an older Spanish presence and with even older indigenous cultural layers. The American presence was to be seen not only directly in the number of Americans active in various public sector agencies but also indirectly in the number of Filipino educators one met who had done their advanced studies in the United States. The Spanish presence was expressed in names of places, in the dominant religious institution, in certain popular sports such as jai-lai, in the designing and administration of towns, and in elites who retained dominance in some industries such as cigar-manufacturing and shipbuilding. The traditional, complex indigenous Malay-Sino presence was expressed in various forms of what the great ethnologist Marcel Mauss called "the techniques of the body" (1960), in games, in food tastes, and in popular music, among other manifestations. In brief, the Philippines was very much a pluralistic society, an interesting test case as a society seeking to modernize itself via industrialization, but still very much agrarian (particularly as one went away from Manila into the interior of Luzon, and beyond to the other islands).

Hence, the study of the occupational structure and the prestige hierarchy of the Philippines is a replication of work which until then had been confined to industrial societies or those having a clear Western ethos. The findings are on the whole consistent with previous studies, but that is not the only message. There are some methodological considerations that the reader will note, for example, having to innovate in the field, particularly in rural areas where respondents are either illiterate or lack everyday familiarity with some modern occupations. At the theoretical level, the responses given as to why occupations are rated the way they are suggested to me that instead of a single dimension of occupational prestige, respondent may actually have plural frames of reference that cannot be reduced to a single "structuralist" position.   This led me to propose in the concluding section (heretofore unpublished[5]) that the evaluation of occupations may be broadly viewed as a dynamic, historical process informed by the four-function paradigm of systems of social action, formulated by Talcott Parsons (1970).

Since the completion of the dissertation, one can safely say that a torrent of pertinent sociological research has flowed under the main occupational stratification bridge.   As Lin and Yauger noted (1975), a watershed was the study of Blau and Duncan (1967) which led to a shift of focus from "the comparative analysis of occupation structure to the study of the process of occupational stratification," (Lin and Yauger 1975: 543), with a host of studies on "status attainment."   The causal model developed by Blau and Duncan became a research paradigm not available at the time of my study, though the reader will find some intergenerational comparisons in the third chapter.   Extensive comparative studies of occupational stratification, providing a much greater range of observations for systematic analysis, have been conducted in the past twenty years in both advanced industrialized and still developing societies.   Perhaps the best known is the work of Donald Treiman (1977; Treiman and Yip 1989), arguing for a convergence theory of occupational differentiation based on the functional imperatives of the modern industrial division of labor, which leads to differentials in power, privilege and prestige.   Treiman's "structural theory of prestige determination" has not gone unchallenged, for example by Cole and Tominaga in examining the Japanese case (1976), and in broader comparative studies of occupational stratification, work structures and social mobility by Kalleberg (1988), Kurz and Muller (1987), Lin and Yauger (1975), Schadee and Schizzerotto (1987) and Simkus (1981).   All of these should be consulted for the reader wishing to be informed as to developments in occupational stratification and social mobility since my study of the Philippines.

Related to the very impressive flourishing of sociological attention given to occupational stratification in the past quarter of a century or so, is the quantitative revolution that has taken place in sociology.   The reader will find in my study mainly descriptive statistics and simple measures of association.   That reflected pretty much the scene of the 1950s. I was fortunate that the IBM 101 had just became available for computational purpose, but this will surely seem like a prehistoric age to researchers today; multiple regression analysis, structural equations and log-linear models were years away from being devised. "Causal inference," so much part of data analysis today (Berk 1988), was simply not part of the statistical training one received then, when the term would have suggested a throwback to unfounded metaphysical speculations of the Nineteenth Century!

THE SOCIAL CONTEXT OF THE STUDY

A sociological study of occupational prestige conducted today in the Philippines (or in any Third World country, for that matter) might well place the research in a broader context of political economy. Socioeconomic differentiation, reflected in the evaluation of occupations, would likely be treated as reflecting or at least interrelated with economic policies of the state and with considerations of power, dominance, and class structures. And the analysis might extend this to see how the occupational structure reflects the position and distortions of the national economy as a function of the country's location in the global economy.

This contextual dimension figures very little in this study, just as the political context of anthropological field studies in colonial settings conducted in the same period was equally muted. Mainstream sociology in the early 1950s gave little attention to political constraints in economic choices, and it was not until much later that the classical writings of Weber and Marx dealing with power, control, and politics became sociologically respectable and even mandatory readings. In an age of sociological innocence, problems of development in the 1950s were seen as socioeconomic without entailing sociopolitical considerations.

Yet, the first two chapters, giving overviews of the Philippines, Central Luzon, and the communities which I investigated, do intimate in several places at the sociopolitical context of the setting. Reference will be found to the problems of increased land tenure, absentee landlordism, and agrarian unrest; passing mention is made in reference to Santo Tomas, one of the four rural communities where I went, to "the dissident activities of the Communist-supported Huk guerrillas." The reader might bear in mind that scholarly, dispassionate documentation on the "Huk" movement (short for Hukbalahap, from Hukbo ng Bayan laban sa Hapon, or People's Anti-Japanese Army) was not available in 1953 to this researcher. Nor was there a comparative analysis of political movements and class conflict in contemporary peasant societies, such as the masterful one of Paige written a generation later (Paige 1975).

The Huks had crested as a menace to the established social order in Central Luzon, but they retained pockets of strength in both Tarlac and Pampanga provinces, the latter the home of the Huk leader Luis Taruc and the province with the highest rate of tenant farming (Kerkvliet 1977:24). Although it does not figure in my description of *poblacion* La Paz, I still remember my first moments walking into town, going inside the Filipino equivalent of a pub, and having the villagers inside nervously draw revolvers in the direction of a stranger who obviously did not belong in this setting. They were relieved (as I was at their relief) to find out that I belonged neither to the Huks nor to the Philippine Constabulary nor to the United States Armed Forces.

The Huks were an agrarian resistance movement, having roots in peasant unrest before Word War II stemming from the practices of a new generation of landlords in Central Luzon who with the American administration adopted a more utilitarian, cash nexus orientation to their tenants growing rice and sugar. As Kessler has noted, by the 1930s the diffuse ties between landlord and peasants that constituted a tacit traditional social contract had broken down (Kessler 1989: 18). The attempt of tenants to mobilize in protest of higher rents and cutbacks in traditional landlord responsibilities came to a halt during the Japanese occupation, with the Huks emerging at the time as vigorous guerrilla opponents to the Japanese, and with various landlords becoming viewed as collaborators. The common front between Huks (also sometimes designated as the National Peasants' Union) and Americans against the Japanese disintegrated, as the post-war, post-independence government of the Philippines became entrenched in traditional elites, including wealthy landlords in Manila. For many years, the Huks received popular support from peasants in Central Luzon whose grievances went unheeded by successive governments.

However, the year that I was in Central Luzon, an important reform figure, Ramon Magsaysay (who had been an effective secretary of defense) was elected on a strong reform ticket. He brought new hopes for reforming the harsh treatment of government troops towards peasant, for providing peasants with agricultural extension services and badly need cash credit, for developing an infrastructure linking the interior with Manila and for other projects helping others than elites (Kerkvliet 1977: 238f). The Huks became isolated or surrendered during an amnesty offered by Magsaysay, and those remaining in the countryside were more predators of peasants in 1953-54 than they were liberators.

My study thus took place during one of the few fortunate periods of post-independence Filipino history: not only was there real economic growth rates but also a widely shared feeling among the populace of political betterment and a more socially just society in the horizon. There were some trouble spots to which my study draws attention: as the reader will note, I observed that the rising proportion of tenant farmers, small size farms and rapidly rising population that could not be supported by the countryside constituted long-term problems. And perhaps apposite is the finding that more persons over 40 felt they were better off than their fathers than did respondents under 40.

Undoubtedly, then, there were clouds in the societal horizon of the Philippines, which at the time I observed less than the famed clouds of Manila sunsets. But both the intellectual climate of "modernization" analysis that was becoming paradigmatic in the social science literature and the buoyant "nation-building" climate of the Philippines combined to make one think that the Philippines was on its way from "underdevelopment" to "development."

What has happened to the social context since this study was completed? Beginning with the tragic and still unexplained air crash that killed Magsaysay in 1957, I am tempted to say there has been spurts of economic growth, giving at least Manila the glitter of modernity (exactly like Teheran under the Shah), but without real social development. Let me in cursory fashion go over some figures and trends.

In comparison to Japan and Korea, two industrial giants in the Far East, GNP per capita of the Philippines has lagged behind during the period 1965-1985 (Table 1 in this section). In fact, the average annual growth rate of 2.3 per cent is less than the average for each category of nations by income level provided by the World Bank (World Bank 1987). In the 1950s and 1960s, Filipino policy seeking industrialization sought to do this via import substitution (Little, Scitovsky, and Scott 1970). The policy led to a sharp increase in the manufacturing sector in the 1950s, with a Gross Domestic Products per capita growth of 3.6 per cent per annum, far ahead of ASEAN countries and South Korea (Villegas 1986: 151). But the growth had flaws, leading to severe regional imbalance, since industrial production was concentrated in Greater Manila (which did benefit my urban community of San Juan del Monte) at the expense of improving agricultural productivity (Villegas 1986: 151; Tidalgo 1988: 140), especially in the staples needed to support a rapidly expanding population. The result was rising unemployment and a greater reliance on imports, unanticipated consequences that accentuated cleavages between social strata. The 1960s and 1970s saw further economic growth being pushed by the Marcos government to promote the ideals of a vaguely defined "New Society." He and his advisers modified the import substitution strategy with a more direct role of the state in domestic and transnational economic development, which one astute observer has described in details as an instance of state capitalism (Stauffer 1985). But it was a small elite class and the military that benefited, in very much the same way as was taking place in other countries whose rulers were strongly backed by the United States, such as Iran under the Shah and Nicaragua under Somoza. Wealth became more concentrated, so that in 1956 the top ten per cent of Filipino families controlled a fourth of the nation's total income, with the figure rising to 37 per cent in the last year of Marcos (Kessler 1989: 17). Writing in 1987, one commentator pointed out that the gap between rich and poor in the Philippines was the widest in Southeast Asia (Burton 1987: 529). Amidst the pauperization of the countryside and the Manila metropolitan area, unemployment and underemployment grew, so that by 1985 it was estimated that 52 per cent of urban dwellers and 62 per cent of rural dwellers lived below the poverty line of $120 per month (Kessler 1989: 17; Burton, 1987: 533).

This took place while Marcos practiced what became widely known as "crony capitalism," allowing a small number of relatives and friends quasi monopolies reminiscent of royal chartered companies, leading to a perverted form of "nationalized" industries

(Villegas, 1986:163; Hawes 1987: 136-38).   Japanese heads of *zaibatsus* and Korean heads of *chaebols* were proposed as models of emulation for Filipino development to rationalize the favoring of intimates of Marcos, but an important aspect of the former two lacking in the latter was a strong sense of identification with collective, national interests and not just personal pursuits. Writing in 1982, Steinberg noted that the the economic aristocracy or oligarchy which depended upon and fronted for multinationals "has, to a startling degree, sold its birthright for a mess of pottage. Individual and group self-interest long has triumphed over notions of the commonweal," (Steinberg 1982:122). The foreign debt of the Philippines soared by 19 per cent a year from 1969-1982, mainly due to increases in government borrowing (Villegas 1986: 168f). Economic growth rates declined in the 1980s, becoming negative in the last two years of the Marcos regime, and external debt service ate up more than one third of the country's foreign currency earnings, which had declined with depressed world prices for Filipino export commodities (Burton 1987: 533).   Worse from a social point of view, wages had been falling since 1968 (Kessler 1989: 25).

The economic crisis of the Philippines developed alongside a political crisis and a no less acute demographic crisis. Demographically, the sharp reduction in the death rate was not matched by a reduction in the birth rate (unlike East Asian NICs, as indicated in the cases of Japan and Korea in Table 1 for the period 1960-1978). When I went to the Philippines in 1953, its population was somewhat in excess of 20 million; five years ago it stood at 55 million, and by the end of the decade it is estimated at about 75 million (World Bank 1987: 254). With a growth rate between 2.5 and 3 per cent, a youthful population over half of whom are under 20, and a government which unlike its predecessor favors a pro-natalist stance, the Philippines today stands almost alone in the Far East facing the Malthusian dilemma, even if political stability were to return tomorrow.

The political crisis became the hallmark of the Marcos regime. Very similar to situations in other countries that promoted economic growth which benefited a small stratum rather than giving rise to a broad new middle class, rural and urban impoverishment and sharp social differentiation in the 1960s gave rise to new protest movements. In 1968, a year marked by global student agitation, radical students and faculty at the University of the Philippines in Manila (Lyons and Wilson 1987: 78)--where I had given a course on social movements during my stay--formed what became the new Communist Party of the Philippines (CPP). They effectively developed a broad-based campaign based on class interests and nationalism, appealing to both middle-class professionals and to landless peasants forgotten in the policies of economic development. Political violence, which I certainly had not observed as part of Filipino culture, became institutionalized in the 1970s with the promotion of the military (much as happened in Iran under the Shah, in Nicaragua under Samoza, and in Guatemala and El Salvador later, among other places), the rise of paramilitary groups and even the formation of death squads (Kessler 1989: 126f). Martial law was declared in September 1972, the constitution was revised and Marcos was fraudulently elected in 1981.

In addition to the Communist insurgency, which had formed a new and more effective military organization than the Huks ever had, there was also a democratic opposition that coalesced around Benigno Aquino and the United Democratic Oppositon (Steinberg 1982). His assassination in 1983 at Manila airport turned out to be a pyrrhic victor for Ferdinand Marcos, since it mobilized opposition at home, including the episcopacy of the Catholic church which threw its resources against the Marcos regime (Lyons and Wilson 1987), and equally important, abroad, particularly in the United States. The result of the crisis of legitimacy of the Marcos regime, despite his attempts to steal the snap elections of February 1986, was his forced exile and the restoration of civilian rule.

To assess what lies ahead for the Philippines for the rest of this decade and beyond is not my endeavor. I have sought to provide the reader with aspects of the situation of the Philippines that may offer her/him with an enhanced perspective for the empirical study I carried out. Let me close by coming back to the question which frames this retrospective reflection. Why hasn't the Philippines become a pacesetter in development in the Far East, or among Third World countries in general? If modernity requires an educated population, the Philippines should long have become a developed society, ahead of others. In 1954, the percentage of its population enrolled in primary, secondary and technical schools stood higher than any other country in all of Asia except Japan and was the same as Canada (United Nations 1957: 83). In 1982 its labor force (the major structure of which is shown in Table 2) showed very high levels of education (Table 3). In 1983, it was in the same category of countries having 201-400 scientists and engineers per 10,000 population as Belgium, Israel, the Netherlands, and Korea, ahead of the United States, Argentina, Australia and Austria (United Nations 1983: 180). So obviously one cannot ascribe the problems of the Philippines to a deficit of human capital.

Some will point to the problems of the Philippines in terms of exogenous factors controlling and exploiting its economy, making it a case of "dependent development" at the hands of American and other foreign multinationals, or international agencies, such as the World Bank and the International Monetary Fund (Broad 1988). In this respect, one could also say that the export sector of the Philippines has not sufficiently diversified beyond commodities, such as sugar and coconut products, which have had a long-term decline in value in world markets.

Others will look inward to economic factors and class conflicts that have distorted industrialization (Schwalbenberg 1989), while still others will consider a still pervasive "colonial mentality" (Constantino 1978) tied to a double tutelage of Spanish and even more, American domination that inhibits Filipino national identity. As an extension of the latter consideration, it might be argued that a "colonial complex" leads to the tacit acceptance of economic dependence on the United States and Japan for investments, and to the very small representation of "native" Filipinos in modern entrepreneurial activities. In a publication stemming from the research (Tiryakian 1959), I drew attention to how very few respondents desired for themselves or for their children to engage in "managerial or executive work" and that this constituted a deficit for a country seeking to become and industrial economy.[6] Table 2 in this essay indicates that the deficit has grown rather than diminished, since in 1984 less than one per cent of the labor force was classified as "proprietors, managers and administrators." I did not at the time set this in a context of "colonial mentality," but certainly today I would support the interpretation of Estanislao (1986) that the ills of the economic crisis of the Philippines do reflect in part a such a mentality. I cannot help but think that one of the major competitive advantages of Japan, which has led it to being a pacesetter, is that it did not have to overcome a "colonial mentality." Equally important, there is a collective pride and national solidarity in Japan that is broader than kin group solidarity, and this seems to have been a feature of the modernizing elites of Japan as much in the Meiji period as in the post-war period. In contrast, belonging to a national group and having national obligations and responsibilities seems much harder to develop much less institutionalize among Filipino elites (Kessler 1989: 22).

I do not pretend to know what remedies will set the Philippines on a better path than the one it has traversed since I conducted my study. The question of building a civil society for collective goals that will provide better standards of living, and this within a democratic framework, is a question of acute concern not only for the Philippines in the post-Marcos period of ambiguity but also in the period of ambiguity facing most societies that have today emerged from an authoritarian past. It would be foolish to think that there may be a single answer, a single model for this. It would be equally foolish and irresponsible for social scientists to shirk coming to grips with the structural and intersubjective challenges of development.

Edward Tiryakian
Durham, N.C., 1990

NOTES

1. Vogel documents this in his widely discussed *Japan As Number One* (1979).

2. By way of comparison, all countries listed as "middle-income" or "upper-middle-income" economies by the World Bank, the two categories of the ASEAN countries, had an average annual growth rate of 1.7 per cent, while "industrial market economies" (including the United States and Japan) had an average rate of 2.3 per cent (World Bank 1987: 204-05).

3. The above remarks should not be construed as upholding the virtue of a "socialist" planned economy model, which was also popular among various Third World countries in the 1960s, but which very recently seems to be rejected across the board.

4. In the 1950s social scientists began to grope for more positive terms to designate non-Western countries. A comprehensive coverage of the categorization used in the post-war period and an explication of the meanings intended would merit a study in itself. "Backward areas" became opprobrious and gave way to "LDCs"--less developed countries; eventually, to still sensibilities, a more diplomatic "developing nations" or "developing societies" was adopted. At the time I wrote up my study, "underdeveloped" was prevalent, and this was years before Andre Gunder Frank gave a new interpretation of "underdevelopment" as not a starting point but as an outcome of "development" (Frank 1967).

5. For published portions of the dissertation, see Tiryakian (1958, 1959).

6. For subsequent complementary studies of entrepreneurship in the Philippines, see Carroll (1963) and Kunio (1985).

REFERENCES

Berger, Peter L. and Hsin-Huang Michael Hsiao. 1988. *In Search of an East Asian Development Model*. New Brunswick, N.J.: Transaction Books.

Berk, Richard A. 1988. "Causal Inference for Sociological Data." Pp. 155-72 in Neil J. Smelser, ed., *Handbook of Sociology*. Newbury Park, CA: Sage.

Blau, Peter M. and Otis Dudley Duncan. 1967. *The American Occupational Structure*. New York: Wiley.

Broad, Robin. 1988. *Unequal Alliance. The World Bank, the International Monetary Fund, and the Philippines*. Berkeley and Los Angeles: University of California Press.

Burton, Sandra. 1987. "Aquino's Philippines: The Center Holds," *Foreign Affairs*, 65 (3): 524-37.

Carroll, John J. 1965. *The Filipino Manufacturing Entrepreneur: Agent and Product of Change*. Ithaca: Cornell University Press.

Cole, Robert E. and Ken'ichi Tominaga. 1976. "Japan's Changing Occupational Structure and its Significance." Pp. 53-96 in Hugh Patrick, ed., *Japanese Industrialization and its Social Consequences*. Berkeley and Los Angeles: University of California Press.

Constantino, Renato. 1978. *Neocolonial Identity and Counter-Consciousness. Essays on Cultural Decolonization*. White Plains, N.Y.: M.E. Sharpe.

Estanislao, Jesus P. 1986. "Economic Relations." Pp. 200-27 in John Bresnan, ed., *Crisis in the Philippines. The Marcos Era and Beyond*. Princeton: Princeton University Press.

Evans, Peter and John D. Stephens. 1988. "Development and the World Economy." Pp. 739-73 in Neil Smelser, ed., *Handbook of Sociology*.

Frank, Andre Gunder. 1967. *Capitalism and Underdevelopment in Latin America*. New York: Monthly Review Press.

Gereffi, Gary and Donald Wyman, eds. 1990. *Manufacturing Miracles: Paths of Industrialization in Latin America and East Asia*. Princeton: Princeton University Press.

Hawes, Gary. 1987. *The Philippine State and the Marcos Regime. The Politics of Export*. Ithaca, N.Y.: Cornell University Press.

Kalleberg, Arne L. 1988. "Comparative Perspectives on Work Structures and Inequality," *Annual Review of Sociology*, 14: 203-25.

Kerkvliet, Benedict J. 1977. *The Huk Rebellion. A Study of Peasant Revolt in the Philippines*. Berkeley and Los Angeles: University of California Press.

Kessler, Richard J. 1989. *Rebellion and Repression in the Philippines*. New Haven: Yale University Press.

Kunio, Yoshihara. 1985. *Philippine Industrialization. Foreign and Domestic Capital*. Quezon City: Ateneo de Manila University Press; Singapore: Oxford University Press.

Kurz, Karin and Walter Muller. 1987. "Class Mobility in the Industrial World," *Annual Review of Sociology*, 13: 417-42.

Lin, Nan and Daniel Yauger. 1975. "The Process of Occupational Status Achievement: A Preliminary Cross-national Comparison," *American Journal of Sociology*, 81 (3): 543-62.

Little, Ian, T. Scitovsky and M. Scott. 1970. *Industry and Trade in Some Developing Countries. A Comparative Study*. London and New York: Oxford University Press.

Lyons, John and Karl Wilson. 1987. *Marcos and Beyond. The Philippine Revolution*. Kenthurst, Australia: Kangaroo Press.

Mauss, Marcel. 1960 (1934). "Les Techniques du Corps." Pp. 363-86 in Mauss, *Sociologie et Anthropologie*. Paris : Presses Universitaires de France.

Moore, Wilbert E. 1951. *Industrialization and Labor. Social Aspects of Economic Development*. Ithaca and New York: Cornell University Press.

Nisbet, Robert A. 1970. "Developmentalism: A Critical Analysis." Pp. 167-204 in John C. McKinney and Edward A. Tiryakian, eds., *Theoretical Sociology. Perspectives and Developments*. New York: Appleton-Century-Crofts/Meredith.

Paige, Jeffery M. 1975. *Agrarian Revolution. Social Movements and Export Agriculture in the Underdeveloped World*. New York: Free Press.

Parsons, Talcott. 1970. "Some Problems of General Theory in Sociology." Pp. 27-68 in John C. McKinney and Edward A. Tiryakian, eds., *Theoretical Sociology. Perspectives and Developments*.

Schadee, H.M.A. and A. Schizzerotto. 1987. "The collective perception of occupational inequalities in contemporary Italy:

multi-dimensional evaluations and one-dimensional scales,"
European Sociological Review, 3 (2): 127-44.

Simkus, Albert A. 1981. "Comparative Stratification and Mobility,"
International Journal of Comparative Sociology, 22 (3-4): 213-36.

Schwalbenberg, Henry M. 1989. "Class Conflict and Economic
Stagnation in the Philippines: 1950-72," *Philippine Studies*, 37
(4): 440-50.

Stauffer, Robert B. 1985. "The Philippines political economy:
(dependent) state capitalism in the corporatist mode." Pp.
241-65 in R. Higgott and R. Robison, eds., *Southeast Asia.
Essays in the Political Economy of Structural Change*. London
and Boston: Routledge & Kegan Paul.

Steinberg, David J. 1982. *The Philippines. A Singular and a Plural
Place*. Boulder, CO: Westview.

Tidalgo, Rosa Linda P. 1988. "Labour Markets, Labour Flows and
Structural Change in the Philippines." Pp. 139-94 in Pang Eng
Fong, ed., *Labour Market Developments and Structural Change
the Experience of ASEAN and Australia*. Singapore: Singapore
University Press.

Tiryakian, Edward A. 1958. "The Prestige Evaluation of Occupations
in an Underdeveloped Country: the Philippines," *American
Journal of Sociology*, 63 (4): 390-9.

_____. 1959. "Occupational Satisfaction and Aspiration in an
Underdeveloped Country: The Philippines," *Economic
Development and Cultural Change*, 7 (4): 431-44.

Touraine, Alain. 1984. *Le retour de l'acteur*. Paris: Fayard.

Treiman, Donald J. 1977. *Occupational Prestige in Comparative
Perspective*. New York: Academic Press.

Treiman, Donald J. and Kam-Bor Yip. 1989. "Educational and
Occupational Attainment in 21 Countries." Pp. 373-94 in
Melvin L. Kohn, ed., *Cross-National Research in Sociology*.
Newbury Park, CA: Sage.

United Nations. 1957. Report on the World Social Situation. New
York.

_____. 1983. 1982 Report on the World Social Situation. New
York.

Villegas, Bernardo. 1986. "The Economic Crisis." Pp. 145-75 in John
E. Bresnan, ed., *Crisis in the Philippines. The Marcos Era and
Beyond*. Princeton; Princeton University Press.

Vogel, Ezra. 1979. *Japan as Number One. Lessons for America.* Cambridge, Mass: Harvard University Press.

Wong, John. 1979. *ASEAN Economies in Perspective.* Philadelphia: Institute for the Study of Human Issues.

The World Bank. 1980. *World Development Report 1980.* New York: Oxford University Press.

_____. 1987. *World Development Report 1987.* New York: Oxford University Press.

Table 1. Philippines, Japan, Korea: Selected Statistics

	Year	Philippines	Japan	Korea
Growth of Production				
GDP	1960-70	5.1%	10.5%	8.5%
	1970-78	6.3	5.0	9.7
	1980-85	-0.5	3.8	7.9
Industry	1960-70	6.0	10.9	17.2
	1970-78	8.6	6.0	16.5
Manufacturing	1960-70	6.7	11.0	17.2
	1970-78	6.8	6.2	18.3
Services	1960-70	5.2	11.7	8.4
	1970-78	5.4	5.1	8.7
Labor Force Composition				
Agriculture	1960	61%	33%	66%
	1978	48	13	41
Industry	1960	15	30	9
	1978	16	39	37
Services	1960	24	37	25
	1978	36	48	22

Urbanization				
Total population	1960	30%	62%	28%
	1980	36	78	55
Population in	1960	27	35	61
cities 500,000+	1980	36	41	77

Education				
Enrollment in higher ed	1960	13%	10%	5%
as % of pop. age 20-24	1976	24	29	11
Enrollment in secondary	1960	26	74	27
school as % of age grp.	1977	56	93	88

Demographic				
crude birth rate/1000	1960	45	18	41
	1978	35	15	21
crude death rate/1000	1960	15	8	13
	1978	9	6	8

Average Wealth				
GNP per capita	1978	$ 510	7,280	1,160
	1985	580	11,300	2,150
Av. annual growth rate	1965-85	2.3%	4.7%	6.6%

Source: The World Bank, *World Development Report 1980*. Washington, D.C. 1980. Figures for 1985 are from The World Bank, *World Development Report, 1987*. Washington, D.C. 1987.

Table 2. Philippines: Percentage Distribution of Employed
        Persons 1956-1984, Selected Occupational Groups

Occupational Group	1956	1968	1984
Total Employed ('000s)	7702	10471	19632
Professional & technical	2.8%	4.9%	5.8%
Proprietors, managers & administrators	4.6	4.4	0.9
Clerical & Sales	7.9	10.1	16.3
Farmers, farm laborers, fishermen, loggers & related	58.8	53.5	49.2
Craftsmen & production process	13.9	13.6	19.4
Service and related	7.0	8.6	7.8

Source: Tidalgo (1988), p. 148.

Table 3. Philippines: Distribution of Labor Force by Highest
          Grade Completed, 1965 and 1982

Level Completed	Labor Force		Employed		Unemployed	
	1965	1982	1965	1982	1965	1982
No schooling	14.2%	5.3%	14.7%	5.4%	6.3%	2.9%
Elementary	61.9	50.4	62.3	51.7	55.2	30.3
High School	15.5	25.6	14.8	25.1	25.9	34.4
College	8.5	18.6	8.2	17.8	12.7	32.3

Source: Tidalgo (1988), p. 152.

ACKNOWLEDGEMENTS (1990)

The original doctoral dissertation filed with the then Department of Social Relations at Harvard University contains a detailed list of persons, both in the United States and in the Philippines to whom the study owes for its inception and implementation. I will not repeat the long list of names here but would like to recall three faculty mentors in particular. John Pelzel, a "scholar's scholar," gave me a great appreciation for the Far East and the complex interplay of tradition and modernity in that part of the world. Peter Rossi, then a young assistant professor and now one of the discipline's distinguished statesmen, not only provided important professional tutelage in survey research and stratification analysis but also warm collegiality in the otherwise daunting Olympian setting of Social relations. Finally, the chairman of my supervisory committee, Talcott Parsons, was and continues to be a prime intellectual influence in my academic career, one who encouraged rather than stifled his students' sociological imagination.

In the preparation of the present volume, I am indebted to Brigitte Neary for helpful bibliographical assistance, and to Susan Brooks, Connie Blackmore, Margaret Lawless and Elizabeth Wing for quality secretarial assistance. Both the original study and the new introduction have benefited from my life-long editor, Dr. Josefina C. Tiryakian.

It is more than appropriate that this study be dedicated to the people of the Philippines, whose generosity and fortitude are exemplary. Victims of physical as well as man-made disasters, they surely deserve a more just society that can harness the great potential of their country.

The Evaluation of Occupations in a Developing Country

The Philippines

CHAPTER I

INTRODUCTION

This study is an endeavor to bring about a convergence between two interrelated sociological problems: a) the evaluation of occupational roles and b) the occupational structure of a society in transition. The evaluational arranging or ranking of occupational roles on the part of societal members is the subject matter of occupational stratification. This in turn relates to the more complex and more general field of social stratification--the hierarchical ranking of social units according to certain criteria, such as wealth, education, family, physical characteristics, and, of course, occupation. It may be mentioned that it is an extremely rare type of social system where all the members of that system are ranked solely on the basis of a single criterion, but the relative weight of one criterion can and has been emphasized in many societies.

Industrial societies, from one aspect, may be characterized by the breakdown of primary group ties (or at least in their relative unimportance in structuring the social situation of adult members), the impersonality of social contacts (i.e., interacting with segments of personalities, rather than with the whole of the individual), and a relatively high degree of spatial, if not social, mobility. In such societies the occupational role of an individual tends to become his primary label of identification to others. Of great psychological

3

and sociological importance is why, given even a rudimentary division of labor, occupational roles tend in all societies to be hierarchically evaluated in relation to one another--why certain jobs are considered more prestigeful and dignified than others. One attempt of this study was to discover what are the frames of reference by which individuals evaluate specific occupational roles.

The second aim of the present research was to study the occupational structure of a country undergoing socio-cultural transition from a rural-agrarian type of society to an urban-industrial one. The Philippines is one of the many underdeveloped areas in the world which are passing through various stages of this transition; in this process these countries (notably in Latin America, many parts of Africa, and Southeast Asia) are profoundly altering their social structure and the patterns of interpersonal behavior to be found therein. It would seem of great sociological relevance to observe such social systems in transition, if one is willing to accept the premise that the complex social order of Western industrial societies represents a form which has evolved from simpler ones. Unfortunately, the laboratory of the social sciences (or any laboratory for that matter) cannot reverse the flow of time in our own historical development, so that to study previous stages of our social order we are at the mercy of often incomplete historical documents and records. But present societies in transition are available for such studies, and they offer rich comparative materials. To study changes in the social structure of a society, it seems that one pertinent focus is the occupational structure of that social system. What new occupations result? How are these new occupational roles evaluated relative to previous existent types? What motivates individuals to enter these new forms of employment, and what adjustments do they have to make in these new conditions? From this starting point one could then go up the ladder of generality and seek to find how changes in the division of labor affect the greater network of social relationships.[1]

The results of this study are to be regarded as only an attempt to establish a basis for such a starting point. Rather than launch on broad theoretical considerations relating occupational stratification to social stratification and the latter to the dynamics of social systems,[2] we shall limit ourselves to presenting the prestige evaluation of certain occupations and selected aspects of the occupational structure of the country under study, the Philippines.

If we can show certain patterns in this evaluation and the relation between these and patterns in industrialized societies, then we might be able to make certain inferences about the sort of changes occurring within this particular society. In turn, these changes might, it is hoped, give us an enlarged perspective about the changes in the occupational structure which have taken place in our own society.

Although it is only within the past thirty years or so[3] that we have had empirical studies of the prestige evaluation of occupational roles, the stratification of societies by occupational groups and the invidious ranking of individuals on the basis of the work they performed was familiar in antiquity. Long before sociology came into existence, Herodotus, a great sociological observer, remarked:

> The Egyptians are divided into seven distinct classes--these are, the priests, the warriors, the cowherds, the swineherds, the tradesmen, the interpreters, and the boatmen. Their titles indicate their occupations. the warriors consist of Hermotybians and Calasirians who . . . are forbidden to pursue any trade, and devote themselves entirely to warlike exercises, the son following the father's calling.
>
> Whether the Greeks borrowed from the Egyptians their notions about trade, like so many others, I cannot say for certain. I have remarked that the Thracians, the Scyths, the Persians, the Lydians, and almost all other barbarians, hold the citizens who practice trades, and their children, in less repute than the rest, while they esteem as noble those such as are given wholly to war. These ideas prevail throughout the whole of Greece, particularly among the Lacedaemonians. Corinth is the place where mechanics are least despised.
>
> The warrior class in Egypt has certain privileges in which none of the rest of the Egyptians participated except the priests, etc.[4]

Other ancient systems of occupational stratification, both theoretical and actual, are to be found in Plato's Republic, in classical Rome,[5] and of course, in India.[6] The latter is a striking illustration of a caste system in which specialization of occupational stratification has always been of major consideration in the functional differentiation of societal members.[7]

The remainder of this section will be devoted to presenting a brief review of more modern studies of occupational stratification (specifically, of empirical studies dealing with the prestige evaluation of occupational roles), and also to sketching features of the historical background and present-day setting of the Philippines which are pertinent to our study.

PREVIOUS STUDIES OF OCCUPATIONAL STRATIFICATION[8]

The first reported empirical study on this subject was the one conducted by Counts[9] in 1925. He gave to students and teachers a list of thirty occupations to rank according to the social standing of each occupation, and he noted with amazement the surprisingly high degree of agreement between both. Ensuing studies in the United States, chiefly using "captive audiences" of college students, also found a very high consensus of agreement between judges and between studies. Even the great economic depression of the 1930s did not materially affect the relative ranking of occupations. All these early studies were conducted on a small segment of the total population of the United States, and it was not until 1947 that a study was published pertaining to the evaluation of occupations based on a national sample.[10]   This report of the National Opinions Research Center, under the supervision of Cecil North and Paul Hatt, involves a sample of 2,920 respondents stratified by geographic location, size of city, age, sex, socio-economic status, and race. Respondents were given a list of 88 distinct occupations, each of which was to be evaluated on a five-point scale according to personal opinions of the general standing of the occupation involved.   The results showed that government officials (U.S. Supreme Court Justice, state governor, mayor of a large city, etc.) had the highest *average* rating, followed by professionals and semi-professionals (physician, scientist, lawyer, etc.) The lowest-rated of these occupations were shoe shiner, street sweeper, and garbage collector--jobs "that imply little or no public responsibility, involve little skill, and are low-paid . . ."[11]   Perhaps the most striking feature of this study was the high agreement among individuals, regardless of socio-economic status, sex, geographical location, etc., as to the ratings of the occupations.[12] The report also points out the criteria used by respondents in evaluating the standing of occupations: income was mentioned most frequently (18 percent of the cases), followed by *service to humanity* or *the essential nature of the job* (16 percent); *social prestige* and *requirements* for the job (education, hard work, or money) were the only other criteria mentioned by more than 10 percent of the respondents.

In summary of the American data, it appears that

> . . . the professions and 'higher' business occupations continue to receive high ranks; the skilled trades, technical occupations and occupations in the distribution field are given intermediate ranks; and the semi-skilled and unskilled occupations are given low ranks.[13]

Cross-cultural studies of the prestige evaluation of occupational roles began to appear after World War II and have been conducted on citizens of such countries as Great Britain,[14] Australia,[15] New Zealand,[16] Japan[17], Germany[18] and the Soviet Union. Although different occupations and different procedures were used, nevertheless, there appears to be striking agreement between the nations reported as to the types of occupational roles which are evaluated. After computing correlation coefficients between each pair of countries as well as the overall degree of consensus, Rossi and Inkeles[19] concluded that:

> . . . our examination of occupational ratings in six modern industrialized countries reveals an extremely high level of agreement, going far beyond chance expectancy, as to the relative prestige of a wide range of particular occupations despite the variety of socio-cultural settings in which they are found.

Thus it appears that in all the empirical cross-cultural studies the professions, high government jobs, and the "top" positions of the industrial system stand high in the prestige hierarchy of occupational roles and that semi-skilled and unskilled occupations stand at the bottom. How can one account for such a high consensus on the part of so many different judges?

One theoretical explanation is the "structuralist" position suggested by Rossi and Inkeles.[20] This view sees the modern industrial order as an integrated system of occupational roles, relatively unaffected by particular cultural patterns and value-systems (of course there will be some variations in the prestige hierarchy arising from cultural differences or from differentials in the presence of industrialization in various countries, but such variation will tend to diminish over time). Once the industrial system becomes established, the traditional rank-ordering of occupations will eventually become a part of the modern industrial society, such that even those forms of employment not constitutive of the industrial order (occupations which may have been highly evaluated by the particular culture) will tend "to have roughly the same standing relative to each other and to other occupations no matter what their national cultural setting.[21]

This "structuralist" position seems open to empirical and theoretical criticisms. First, implicitly it accepts that there is a single prestige hierarchy in any given industrialized society and that the primary focus of this hierarchy is centered on the industrial order. Hatt, on the other hand, analyzed the data of the previously mentioned NORC study and reached the conclusion that meaningful comparisons of prestige are only applicable to occupations located *within* a certain organically related group or "situs."[22] Inter-situs judgements, he argued, may not be meaningful to respondents and hence do not have the consistency and legitimacy of intra-situs evaluations.

It can be further argued that the industrial system is but one aspect of the economy, which is in turn but one aspect of the larger social system. For there to be a single prestige hierarchy one would have to adopt the radical and theoretically unjustifiable position that *all* occupations derive their functional significance from either the economy or the industrial system. If this is so, where does that leave the teacher, the minister, the policeman, and government officials, to name a few non-industrial occupations?

Furthermore, even if one accepts the paramount importance of the industrial order, certain empirical considerations have to be explained. Why is it that in the six countries discussed by Rossi and Inkeles professionals (notably physician, scientist, university professor) and high government officials consistently rate higher than the highest positions of the industrial order (such as company director, factory director, etc.)? It seems equally justifiable to advance the position that the occupations of the industrial order are subsumed under the traditional prestige hierarchy of a given society as vice versa.

One last criticism must be entertained in connection with this "structuralist" position. No consideration is made of the subjective frames of reference by which respondents evaluate occupational roles. If there is such a thing as a single prestige hierarchy which becomes subsumed under the industrial order, then the frames of reference should also reflect a monolithic structure, regardless of the country studied. By and large, one might assume, the paramount frame of reference of judges should be an economic one since the paramount focus of the industrial system is located in the economy sector of the society. If, on the other hand, one finds in a given industrialized society a plurality of frames of reference in evaluating the prestige status of occupational roles, then one might argue against a single prestige hierarchy. The empirical evidence, as Davies points out,[23] is not clear-cut due to the failure of most previous studies to collect "subjective reports" from respondents presented with a ranking task. However, one may compare the frames of reference found in the American study done by the National Opinion Research Center with the Australian study reported by Tuft. Below is contrasted the frames of reference in the rank order of importance mentioned by American and Australian respondents:[24]

United States	Australia
1. income	1. intelligence/education required
2. service to humanity	2. interest of work
3. prerequisites for job (education, hard work, money)	3. importance to community
4. social prestige of job	4. independence (being your own boss)
5. high moral standards, honesty, responsibility required	5. possibility of advancement
6. requisites for job (intelligence, ability)	6. security
7. security, steady work	7. working conditions
8. good future: such jobs not overcrowded; possibility of advancement	8. income
9. working conditions	
10. independence	

Comparing the two, one is impressed with the similar frames of reference found but also with some major differences in the rank order, notably income, independence, and possibility of advancement. To an extent, meaningful comparison is vitiated by the fact that the lists of occupations used in both countries were not identical. For the time being one can only point to the pressing need of investigating the subjective aspect of occupational evaluation.[25] Of major theoretical consideration is the fact (as will be shown later by our Philippine data) that not only do different respondents have different frames of reference, but that the same individual may rank occupations on the basis of different status-systems.

Evaluating the results of previous empirical studies is both a simple and an arduous task. On the one hand is the striking agreement, regardless of various indices, within and between countries as to the prestige evaluation of broad occupational groups (professionals, managerial and executive, manual workers, etc.). On the other hand the significance of this agreement has not been pursued in a general theoretical context, and the reliability of thisagreement is blurred by the variety of techniques used in obtaining the prestige status of occupational roles.[26]

Reversing the law of entropy, the writer is committed to the belief that out of chaos comes order. However, we feel that the present state of sociological studies of occupational stratification is still in a primordial era of chaos and obscurity but that the dawn of order is in the not-so-distant future.

THE PHILIPPINES

A word might be said to justify the present study, since we have previously indicated that there already exists a substantial number of empirical investigations on occupational stratification. In a certain sense, previous studies represent a biased sample. They have been conducted on countries that either share a common Anglo-Saxon cultural tradition (the United States, Great Britain, New Zealand, Australia) or a high level of industrialization and urbanization (Japan and Germany)[27], or both. Furthermore, the social system in all these countries has been in the main relatively stable for quite some time; related to this is that each nation has on the whole a fairly homogeneous culture. None of these countries could be called a "primitive" society or even an "underdeveloped" nation; moreover, the samples in these studies were heavily drawn from urban areas so that little generalization can be made about rural-agrarian communities.

The Philippines, as will be shown shortly, is a striking contrast to the other countries studied. It has a plurality of co-existing and contrasting socio-cultural systems. The main basis of the economy is agricultural rather than industrial. It has a high growth potential and a rapidly expanding population. These and other factors make it highly atypical of previously reported societies, so that we are here presented with an interesting test case: how similar or dissimilar are the patterns of occupational prestige?

Before we can begin to answer this crucial question, we shall briefly sketch for the reader the historical development of the Philippines and a description of some salient features of present conditions. In succeeding chapters we shall describe the setting of this study, the methodological procedures used, the composition and characteristics of our sample, aspects of the occupational structure as revealed by our respondent, the prestige evaluation of occupational roles, and a comparison of the latter with previously published findings.

History of the Philippines[28]

Long before the arrival of Magellan in 1521, the Philippines were actively engaged in commercial relations with other areas in the Orient such as China, Java, and Borneo, to mention a few. Successive waves of immigration from the north, west, and south had populated the Philippines with a diversity of racial and cultural types. In prehistoric times the Philippines was connected by land bridges to Southeastern Asia, and a race of short people (sometimes referred to as pygmies) came across from the mainland. After the retreat of the last great ice cap which formerly covered the northern hemisphere, great upheavals caused the separation of the Philippines from the continent and the formation of its numerous islands which today are over seven thousand in number. During the New Stone Age large bands of invaders called "Indonesians" came over from the mainland (not from Indonesia) and settled in various parts. Later, Malays who had spread from the Malay peninsula to islands south of the Philippines, such as Sumatra and Borneo, migrated to the north. Although for the most part they settled in the southern regions of the Philippines (the Sulu Archipelago, Mindanao, etc.), some even penetrated into the northernmost parts, such as Luzon. The Malays were influenced by the civilizations of India and China and brought elements of both cultures with them; from the eighth to the fourteenth centuries of the Christian era the Philippines was under the influence of two great Hindu-Malayan empires, the Sri-Viṣaya and the Madjapahit. By the fourteenth and fifteenth centuries the Madjapahit empire was subjugated by a new force, Islam, and a great many Malays in the Philippines became converted to the faith of Islam. When the Spaniards arrived on the scene in the sixteenth century, the Muslims were seeking to establish their supremacy over the whole of the Philippines.

Before we terminate with Filipino history prior to the Spanish conquest, it may be of interest to note the influence of China and Japan. Both had been actively involved in trade with the coastal areas of the Philippines, and the southern Filipino port of Cebu was an important commercial center. On the less peaceful side, the Philippine coastal areas were often subject to attack by Chinese and Japanese pirates who on occasion even attempted large-scale invasions. From about the twelfth century onward, many Chinese came not only as traders but also as settlers; their astuteness in economic affairs gave them an advantage which they have never relinquished (today about 90 per cent of the retial and wholesale trade is controlled by the Chinese) but at the same time made them an object of hostility and suspicion, especially since they retained close ties with the Chinese mainland.

Economically, the Philippines before the Spanish conquest was more prosperous than today. Rice was then (and still is) the main item in the diet, but unlike today was plentiful enough for the population and did not have to be imported from other countries to meet a deficit; other staple crops were sugar cane, coconuts, and hemp (from which cloth was woven). Fishing and shipbuilding were major industries, made possible by an abundant supply of timber. Weaving of cotton and silk was extensive and cloths were profitable export products, along with pearls and metalwork.

Politically, however, the Philippines had very little cohesion. When the Spanish conquistadores arrived on the scene in the latter part of the sixteenth century, they found"no established native states but rather a congeries of small clan-like groups, the headship of which was hereditary."[29]

Superior weapons and military tactics, combined with a lack of unified defense on the part of the natives, enabled the Spaniards to conquer the northern islands. But the Spaniards were never able to subjugate the fierce Muhammedan Moros living in southern areas such as Mindanao; the latter frequently launched predatory raids against the northern coastal areas as far north as Manila and devastated the countryside. To this day there is still an uneasy tension between the Christian Filipinos of the north and the Muslim Moros in the south.

Although for a short period the Spaniards encouraged trade between the Philippines and other nearby countries, they soon adopted a more restrictive policy which stifled economic development. In 1591 Spain closed down the trade between the Philippines and South America, and for more than 200 years after the external trade was limited to two ships annually sailing to and from Mexico (the Acapulco galleons). Internally, the native industries were severely disrupted by a combination of factors.

The Spanish practice of the *repartimiento*, or drafting of Filipinos for employment on public works, took the workers away from their accustomed occupations and caused the abandonment of many industries.[30]

Often this led to the severe diminution of manpower needed for agricultural pursuits, a consequence being a dwindling food supply. The Spaniards, needing ships for their own commercial and military activities, pushed the shipbuilding trade to the detriment of other industries. Skilled carpenters and other workers were forced to relocate and lived under very arduous conditions, made even more perilous by the frequent raids of the Moros in search of captives to build their own ships. On the other hand, it must be kept in mind that the Spanish conquest, at least in its ideology, was essentially a missionary one.

Commercial pursuits were secondary to converting natives to Christianity and to their leading a religious life. The Spaniards sought to prevent the exploitation of natives by trading posts (in contrast to North America), and thus the Filipinos were tacitly allowed to lead an idle life. Moreover, since whatever material wealth the Filipinos had might be seized by under-paid Spanish soldiers and greedy *encomenderos* (supervisors of large grants of land or *encomiendas*), even the Spanish friars advised the people to neglect their industries for their own welfare.

Previous to the arrival of the Spaniards, the social stratification had three broad levels: nobility, commoners, and slaves. On the whole, Spanish rule had little effect on the local structure. The Spanish government was patterned along the lines of the Spanish colonies in America. At the head of the political hierarchy was the governor-general who presided over the *audiencia*, essentially an appellate court of justice which also advised the governor-general in administrative and legislative matters. Under him were the provincial heads, or *alcaldes-mayores* who had broad executive and judicial functions. Each province was divided into *pueblos* (roughly equivalent to townships or municipalities) directed by *gobernadorcillo* (elected annually by a restricted electorate of the *pueblo*). At this territorial level the pre-Spanish local government was left unchanged. The old nobility class produced the village chiefs who preserved their former authority, administered justice, collected taxes, and served as go-betweens for the village and spanish religious and civil bodies. These chiefs, called *caciques*, formed the native aristocracy and the backbone of Spanish indirect rule; meek before the Spanish officials, they ruled their communities with an iron hand.

On the Spanish side it may be mentioned that there was a scarcity of qualified administrators. Inadequate salaries and the long distance from Spain made the recruitment of competent officials problematical [31]; those who came were often given to graft and corruption. *Faute de mieux*, the friars often took over the more important civil functions, and in hundreds of villages the only Spaniard present was the priest. Rather than teach his parishioners Spanish, the friar found it easier to learn the native dialect, so that throughout the Spanish period the teaching of Spanish was greatly restricted.

With the curtailment of external trade (wine and tobacco were government monopolies), agriculture was the most important economic activity. Basically, there were four classes of land proprietors:[32]

1. religious corporations (members of the corporation cultivated their lands or rented them out to tenants)
2. individual Spaniards, the recipient of land grants
3. mestizos and natives (who often had hired workers)
4. small independent landholders who cultivated their own soil

Of these, the religious corporations or orders (Dominicans, Augustinians, Recoletos) had the greatest assets. By the end of the Spanish rule they possessed over 400,000 acres; over half of their holdings was in the Manila area which alone had more than 60,000 tenants on the estates of the clergy![33] The religious and economic power of the priesthood often placed it in political conflict with the State as to which should have ultimate power in the Philippines--a conflict never completely resolved by the Spaniards.

When Spain lost her American colonies during the first half of the nineteenth century, she came to pay increasing attention to the Philippines. The former mercantilistic theory was abandoned in favor of encouraging and expanding commerce. Ports were opened up to foreign trade, banking facilities were developed, foreign firms were allowed to do business inside the Philippines, transportation and communication were expanded; all this was marked by an improvement in the standard of living and a rise in the population. At the same time, by coming into contact with the rest of the world, Filipinos also became aware of political events and new ideas spreading through Europe and America. Agitation for political reforms spread with increasing intensity during the second half of the century, but, with minor exceptions, the demanded concessions for greater independence were not forthcoming from Madrid. By the 1880s and 1890s such figures as Rizal, del Pilar, Bonifacio, and Aguinaldo, to name a few, were inflaming the spirit of Filipino freedom. Anti-clerical feelings, partly due to the despotism and economic wealth of the friars, partly due to the subordination of Filipino secular priests to Spanish friars, were also spreading, and with this came the rise of Masonry.[34] With the spread of these *filibusterismos* ("subversive ideas"), came harsh acts of retaliation on the part of the Spaniards, which only served to heighten the tension to the breaking point. This culminated in armed encounters between Filipino revolutionaries of the Katipunan secret society and regular Spanish troops during the month of August 1896 in the vicinity of Manila; the governor-general declared a state of martial law, and the War of Independence was on. By 1898 the Spaniards (greatly handicapped by having to send troops to Cuba to put down the rebellion there) had lost most of the Philippines and the *coup de grace* was administered by the naval expedition of Admiral Dewey. On January 23, 1899, the Filipino independence movement was climaxed with the proclamation of the first constitutional Philippine Republic; but on February 6, 1899, the American Senate ratified the Treaty of Paris which, in part, ceded the Philippines to the United States. The Filipinos greatly resented the American occupation, which they considered to be a betrayal, and again fought for their independence.[35]

By 1901, however, the American army was completely victorious, and on July 4, 1901, William Howard Taft, later President of the United States, became the first American governor-general. The United States, nevertheless, was committed to ultimately granting the Philippines independence and pursued this policy gradually. In 1902 a civil government was established by order of President Theodore Roosevelt. In 1907 the first Philippine Assembly was elected, and with it came increasing self-government. On November 15, 1935, the Philippines was given Commonwealth status, and finally on July 4, 1946, achieved complete political freedom, after having to suffer through trying years of an unexpected Japanese occupation, the ravages of which made Manila the second most devastated city during World War II after the Polish capital of Warsaw.[36] Thus in the fifty years between 1896 and 1946 the Philippines saw the occupation of three foreign powers before it could accomplish political independence!

Before turning to the present-day setting of the Philippines, let us see some of the effects of the American regime. Of primary importance was the tremendous spread of public education, helped in 1901 by the arrival of 1,000 American teachers who within a decade made English spoken by more people than Spanish. By 1939 there were over 11,000 schools in the Philippines where there had been less than 1,000 in 1900; the school population rose in the same period from less than 100,000 to over 1,750,000![37] Public health measures greatly cut down the death rate by bringing under control smallpox, cholera, and bubonic plague; this together with the reduction of infant mortality enabled the Philippines to double its population in forty years.

Politically, a system of administering justice impartially and maintaining law and order helped to really unify the country.[38]

Religious tolerance was written into the constitution and the separation of Church and State became an accepted principle. The development of scientific and literary pursuits, previously blocked by the Spanish clergy, were greatly encouraged. Transportation and communication facilities were enlarged. Agricultural production was stimulated in many ways, such as new machineries, rural credit, and irrigation systems. Free trade between the United States and the Philippines was established with the result that three-fourths of the Philippines' exports were being sent to our country, and in return we supplied that country with more than two-thirds of her imports. This economic dependence on the United States has not been altogether beneficial in the long run, however. Instead of seeking new world markets and diversifying her industries, the Philippines during and since the American occupation has relied on exporting traditional commodities such as hemp, tobacco, coconut products (chiefly copra) and sugar, with the bulk going to the United States in return for manufactured goods of all sorts. One result of this has been an unfavorable balance of trade.

To make a broad generalization, the Philippines quickly absorbed American material culture, but the Spanish and pre-Spanish influences left deeper roots (especially in such matters as religion, recreation and social customs, to name a few).

The Philippines Today

Three broad racial divisions are to be found: Negritos, Indonesians, and Malays. The former two are gradually disappearing and do not play a significant role in the present-day setting. The third is usually subdivided into three religious strata: Pagan Malays (Bontoks, Ifugaos, Igorots, and Tinggians of Northern Luzon), Muslim Malays (Moros of Mindanao and Sulu), and Christian Malays (Tagalogs, Visayans, Ilocanos, Bicola, Pampangans, Pangasinans, Zambals). Indonesians and Malays are classified by the Philippine Bureau of Census as belonging to the Brown race, which collectively accounted for 99 per cent of the population in the 1948 census.[39]

Linguistically, the picture is much more complex; there are 87 separate native languages and dialects throughout the islands, and it is not uncommon for adjacent provinces and even municipalities to speak different tongues.   In addition, Spanish is spoken by an aristocratic elite, English is the accepted *lingua franca* of commercial and government circles, and Chinese is also important due to the control of the Chinese in the retail trade.

A unifying factor in all this diversity is the predominance of the Roman Catholic faith, to which three out of four Filipinos belong.   The breakdown of the population by religious denomination at the time of the 1939 census was as follows:[40]

Religion	Number of Persons
Roman Catholic	12,603,365
Aglipayan	1,573,608
Mohammedan	677,903
Protestant	378,361
Buddhist	47,852
Pagan and all other	719,214

The Aglipayan Church, it may be noted, represents a movement which broke off from Catholicism during the War of Independence against Spain.   It was started by Filipinos who objected to the appointment of Spanish-born clerics and who wished to have Filipino clergy and Filipino bishops.   It made much headway in the early part of this century, but the lack of aggressive leadership in recent years has made its influence diminish, especially since the Catholic Church has increasingly appointed Filipinos to high posts in the hierarchy.

Demographically, two facts are of interest.   First is the tremendous rate of natural increase, due to the reduction of infant mortality and the spread of public health measures. With an annual rate of increase of over two per cent, the population is doubling every generation: in 1903 it stood at about 7,500,000, and fifty years later it was over 20,000,000![41]   In 1948 nearly half of the population (over nine million persons) was living on the island of Luzon, and another third was concentrated in the islands of Mindanao, Panay, Negros and Cebu.[42]

Second, it should be noted that 75 per cent of the population lives in non-urban areas (an urban area being defined as having 2,500 or more persons), although there has been a marked movement from rural to urban areas since World War II. [43]   The Philippines is, therefore, chiefly an agrarian society, much as it has been throughout its history.   But today it is faced with acute economic problems which did not previously manifest themselves. Let us see what some of these are.

Perhaps the greatest dilemma is the population surplus coupled with an economy which is unable to absorb the extra manpower, thus causing in recent years a high level of underemployment and unemployment not only in urban areas but in rural areas as well. In their study of nine *barrios* (villages) in Central Luzon, Rivera and McMillan[44] found over one-third of the labor force unemployed and an additional third working 30 hours a week or less (underemployed). With most of the population increase occurring in rural areas, population pressure has caused a shrinkage in the size of individual farms; today nearly 50 per cent of all farms in the Philippines are under two hectares (1 hectare=2.47 acres) and only about 15 per cent have five hectares or more.[45]

In 1952 the national income of the Philippines amounted to a little over seven billion pesos ($3,500,000 at the official rate of exchange), 43 per cent of which came from agriculture.[46] Of all forms of investment, land is the most profitable for several reasons: (a) high rentals, (b) low taxes, often uncollected, (c) low wages paid to the tillers of the soil, (d) high interest rates charged to tenants, and (3) a growing population which needs land and agricultural produce.[47] In general, areas of greatest productivity are also areas of highest land tenure. In Central Luzon, the rice granary of the Philippines, farm tenancy increased between 1948 and 1954 from 60 per cent to over 82 per cent; in the same period, for all regions, the increase was from 37 per cent to over 53 per cent. Absentee landlordism, so familiar in pre-Communist China and other Asiatic countries, is prevalent throughout Luzon and has been the cause of agrarian unrest and agitation, which assumed serious proportions in the late 1940s and early 1950s. Primitive methods of production and the high cost of farm capital result in low acreage yield so that tenants have little surplus to sell, after having to turn over to landlords from 30 to 50 per cent of the harvest. One study showed that in compensation for over 40 days of labor needed to produce one hectare of palay (unhulled rice), tenants and their family members received an average total of only two pesos a day.[48] To purchase grain and essential commodities, the tenant is obliged to borrow credit at high rates of interest form the landlord. The result is a very low and inadequate standard of living. What is needed to broaden the bases of rural economy, as Spencer suggests,[49] is the development of small-scale local industries and the growth of commercialized handicrafts. But even these will only be partial remedies. The two crucial problems, in the opinion of the writer, are land tenure (and the grossly unequal distribution of income between tenant and landlord), and the greatly expanding population.[50]

To delineate with any degree of accuracy the social classes in the Philippines is almost an impossible task. But through talks with various observers, reenforced by personal impressions, the writer would like to suggest the following tentative figures:[51]

Social Class	% of the population
Upper	5
Middle	10
Lower	85

In the upper class (using wealth and "style of living" as rough criteria) one finds professionals (chiefly lawyers, doctors, dentists, university professors), a few commercial leaders, and those who own land and large estates (sugar cane and coconut plantation owners, along with owners of farms); the upper class has the greatest concentration of Spanish-speaking persons, although an increasing percentage of professionals is American-trained. The middle class contains minor government officials, primary and secondary school teachers, clerical workers, and those with small businesses. Finally, in the lower class is to be found the great majority of the population: all manual workers and most of the agricultural workers.[52]

The Philippines presents marked contrasts: great *haciendas*, some the size of large American counties, and masses of poor farm tenants; fertile soils with low productivity; the need for crop diversification together with the emphasis on a single crop cultivation; a relatively unexpanding economy together with a huge excess of births over deaths; high population densities with great tracts of unsettled land; urban centers having movie theatres displaying the latest American films five minutes away from cockpits where cockfighting is still the national pastime; swank residential dwellings side by side with squatters' huts made of makeshift materials--these and countless other examples are the vivid opposites found in the Philippines.

Central Luzon, where the present study was conducted, exemplifies all these contrasts. The Central Plains of Luzon are the greatest producer of palay (unhulled rice), and sugar cane also grows abundantly; in this region one finds the highest percentage of land tenancy--often 100 per cent of the agricultural workers in many communities do not own the land they cultivate. The rural population during the years 1918-1948 increased by 73 per cent, which was less than the national increase of 87 per cent,[53] but this relatively smaller increment is accounted by the rural-urban migration, with the majority going to Manila and its suburbs. Although predominantly an agricultural region, Central Luzon, especially Manila and its suburbs, is also the scene of growing industrialization.[54] It has a diversity of occupational roles and has been subject to various cultural influences. All in all, it appeared to the writer that this area would provide interesting comparison material for the study of occupational stratification.

NOTES

1. It will be obvious to the reader that this is no great insight but merely an echo of the attempts to do just this by such great nineteenth-century sociologists as Spencer and Durkheim.

2. The writer is aware of only two general theoretical formulations on this matter, namely P.A. Sorokin's "Occupational Stratification," Ch. 6 in his *Social Mobility* (New York and London: Harper & Bros., 1927), and Talcott Parsons' "The Problem of Hierarchical Prestige-Ordering of Occupational Roles" (memorandum, Harvard University).

3. Dating back to the pioneer work of G.S. Counts, "The Social Status of Occupations," *School Review*, 1925.

4.   Herodotus, *The Persian Wars*, Bk. II, Chaps. 164-68, trans. by George Rawlinson, in F.R.B. Godolphin, *The Greek Historians*, v. I (New York: Random House, 1942).

5.   See Emile Levasseur, *L'organisation des métiers dans l'Empire Romain* (Paris: V. Giard & E. Briere, 1899). Levasseur's tomes on the history of the French working classes are also relevant.

6.   For a justification of the Indian caste system, see *The Laws* (or *Institutes*) *of Manu*; see also R.C. Majumdar, H.C. Raychaudhuri, and K. Datta, *An Advanced History of India* (London: Macmillan and Co., Ltd., 1950), esp. p. 131 ff.

7.   For other examples of occupational stratification in older societies, see, for example, Emile Durkheim, *De la division du travail social* (Paris: Felix Alcan, 1902), p. 269 *et passim*; also, P. Sorokin, op. cit., p. 100.

8.   The writer will not try to present here an exhaustive summary of all the numerous work on this subject, but will only select same of the more relevant ones. For extensive reviews and bibliographies, see, for example, A.F. Davies, "Prestige of Occupations," *British Journal of Sociology*, III (2): 234-47 June 1952); also, Donald G. MacGee, "Social Stratification," *Current Sociology*, II (1), 1955-54, the whole issue being devoted to stratification.

9.   Counts, *op. cit.*

10.   National Opinion Research Center, "Jobs and Occupations: A Popular Evaluation," *Opinion News*, v. IX (Sept. 1, 1947): 3-13. The full report is entitled "National Opinion on Occupations" (mimeo, University of Denver, April 1947).

11.   *National Opinion on Occupations*, p. 6.

12.   Of course, some variations were found, but these were, by and large, of minor nature.

13.   M.E. Deeg and D.G. Paterson, "Changes in Social Status of Occupations," *Occupations*, XXV (1947): 205-08.

14.   John Hall and D. Caradog Jones, "The Social Grading of Occupations," *British Journal of Sociology*, I (1): 31-55 (March 1950).

15.   Ronald Taft, "The Social Grading of Occupations in Australia," *British Journal of Sociology*, IV (2): 181-88 (June 1953).

16.   A.A. Congalton, "The Social Grading of occupations in New Zealand," *British Journal of Sociology*, IV (1): 45-60 (March 1953).

17.   Research Committee, Japan Sociological Society, *Report of a Sample Survey of Social Stratification in the Six Large Cities of Japan* (Tokyo, 1952).

18.   The German and Russian data are not yet published in English but the main findings are indicated in P. Rossi and A. Inkeles "Gross National Comparisons of Occupational Ratings," *American Journal of Sociology*, LXI (4): 329-39 (January 1956).

19.   *op. cit.*

20.   op. cit., p. 329, 339. This "structuralist" position is not to be confused with that of structural-functional analysis.

21.   *ibid.*, p. 329.

22.   Paul Hatt, "Occupation and Social Stratification," *American Journal of Sociology*, LV (6): 533-42 (May 1950).

23.   *op. cit.*, p. 144.

24.   In some cases the reasons listed are paraphrased from the original text in order to make comparisons easier, but the essential meaning has been preserved.

25. Perhaps the best analysis in this respect is the study of John D. Campbell, *Subjective Aspect of Social Status* (Ph.D. thesis, Harvard University, 1952).

26. Campbell, *op. cit.*, mentions that at least five different methods have been employed in this task:
    1. the rank ordering of a set of listed occupations
    2. the use of the Bogardus social distance technique (e.g., would you like your daughter to marry a carpenter, would you invite an engineer to your home, etc.)
    3. the use of an occupational check list whereby occupational prestige is given by an examination of the relative frequency of the selection of an occupation on the basis of respect
    4. the method of paired comparisons: each occupation to be rated is shown paired with every other occupation, and the respondent gives his preference for each pair
    5. the rating procedure of using a fixed number of categories of differentiated prestige (e.g., excellent, good, fair, etc.)
       (As will be discussed in Chapter III, the present study used the first method.)

27. The Japanese sample drew heavily from respondents living in the six largest cities of Japan. The Russian sample consists of refugees from the Soviet Union who were interviewed by the Russian Research Center of Harvard University; since their former socio-economic background, geographical origin, and other personal data are not given, some question arises as to how representative they are of residents of the Soviet Union. Without making any value judgement, one may consider these persons who fled the USSR as being malintegrated in the dominant social system.

28. Unfortunately we cannot do adequate justice to the historical development since this would take us far off course. For a more systematic treatment of this subject see the following: Emma H. Blair and James A. Robertson, *The Philippine Islands, 1493-1898*, 55

volumes (Cleveland: Arthur H. Clark Co., 1908); Conrado Benitez, *History of the Philippines*, rev. ed., (Boston: Ginn and Company, 1954); P. Reyes, M. Grau-Santamaria, H.O. Beyer, and J.C. de Veyra, *Pictorial History of the Philippines* (Quezon City, P.I., 1953). Other references may be found in the bibliography.

29. "Philippine Islands," *Encyclopedia Britannica*, XIth ed., (1911), p. 397.

30. Benitez, *op. cit.*, p. 51.

31. See Antonio de Morga, *Sucesos de las Islas Filipinas* (new edition by W.E. Retana, Madrid, 1910).

32. E.M. Alip, *Political and Cultural History of the Philippines* (Manila: Alip and Brion Publications, Inc., 1949), p. 35.

33. Benitez, *op. cit.*, p. 358.

34. The first lodges were organized in 1890 and the movement quickly expanded throughout the islands (Benitez, *op. cit.*, p. 260).

35. Cf. Chapter II, p. 41.

36. Even today (1956) Manila still has many shell-torn and bullet-riddled buildings. The old walled section of Intramuros lies in utter ruin, and in the bay can be seen protruding from their watery grave the rusty hulls of Japanese ships sunk during the invasion of Luzon in 1944.

37. Benitez, *op. cit.*, p. 339 f.

38. In 1915 the Sultan of Sulu agreed to relinquish political sovereignty while retaining religious leadership over his Muslim followers.

39. The remainder was distributed as follows: Yellow (Chinese, Japanese, Korean), .5 per cent; White (American, Europeans, Arabs), .1 per cent; Negrito, .1 per cent; Mixed, .3 per cent.

40. Adapted from the Census of the Philippines, 1939, v. II, p. 384.

41. G.F. Rivera, and R.T. McMillan, *The Rural Philippines* (Manila: United States Mutual Security Agency, 1952), p. 102.

42. J.E. Spencer, *Land and People in the Philippines* (Berkeley and Los Angeles: University of California Press, 1954), p. 40.

43. Manila, for example, has nearly doubled its pre-war population, from about 600,000 in 1939 to over a million inhabitants today.

44. G.F. Rivera and R.T. McMillan, *An Economic and Social Survey of Rural Households* in Central Luzon (Manila: U.S.A. Operations Mission to the Philippines, 1954), p. xi.

45. Rivera and McMillan, *The Rural Philippines*, p. 42.

46. Fourth Annual Report of the Central Bank of the Philippines (Manila, 1952).

47. *The Philippines, Agricultural Land Tenure Study* (Manila: U.S. Operations Mission, 1954), p. 15.

48. *loc. cit.*

49. *op. cit.*, p. 14.

50. Unlike India, which is trying to cope with the latter by the spread of birth control techniques, the Philippines Government is unwilling to deal with the population problem due to the opposition of the Catholic Church against any curtailment of family size.

51. This does not include the Chinese, whose contacts with Filipinos are mainly commercial. Although mostly Catholics, they have kept their own customs, maintained their language, educated their children in their own schools. The bulk of the Chinese can be said to belong to the middle class.

52. After heated opposition, the government passed a Minimum Wage Law in 1952 which guarantees urban workers a daily wage of two dollars. Not only are rural workers left unprotected, but also the law is often evaded in the cities--even so, during the writer's stay in the Philippines (1954-55) there was much talk about repealing the law, supposedly because employers cut down their labor force, causing unemployment. Given the high cost of living in urban centers, especially in Manila, any worker capable of supporting his family on the minimum wage must be considered a financial wizard. The strength of family ties is used by city workers to obtain food supplies from relatives in the provinces.

53. Rivera and McMillan, *An Economic and Social Survey*, etc., p. 10.

54. However, heavy industry is still in the neophyte stage. In 1952 the manufacturing industries in the Philippines accounted for only 14 per cent of the national income, but this figure is bound to rise. See, *Industrial Philippines: A Cross Section* (Manila: Philippine Council for United States Aid and U.S. Foreign Operations Administration, 1953).

CHAPTER II

THE URBAN AND RURAL SETTING

For the purpose of this study, it was thought necessary that the total sample should comprise rural as well as urban respondents. Including rural persons seemed desirable because previous studies of occupational stratification focused primarily on urban respondents; furthermore, the majority of Filipinos live in rural-agricultural areas. In selecting an urban community, proximity to the University of the Philippines at Quezon City (near Manila) was a desideratum; our interviewers were students at the university, and the field office for the survey was set up at the Social Science Research Center of the same institution. Manila, with a population of over a million, seemed too large and atypical of urban communities, just as New York City is not usually considered representative of American urban centers.

Several urban sites in the suburbs of Manila were visited by the writer, and after many consultations with Filipinos and Americans acquainted with the region, the municipality of San Juan del Monte was selected. It seemed to be a fairly prosperous community, with diverse forms of economic enterprise; it had a substantial proportion of wealthy homes, but it also had some very poor districts; it was near enough to Manila and Quezon City, and yet had or seemed to have a cachet of its own.   Following this decision, the writer contacted the City Hall of San Juan, and received its wholehearted cooperation in this project.   The mayor and the municipal secretary made available all the pertinent statistical records; they also put the writer in contact with several of San Juan's leading citizens.   Two of the town's oldest and most prominent figures, Don Ramon Fernandez, ex-Senator and former Minister to the Court of St. James, and Señor Jose Artiaga, formerly city engineer of Manila and one of the first Filipinos to get a degree at an American university, gave freely of their time to enable the writer to get an historical perspective on the changes that have occurred in San Juan in the last sixty years or so.

Señor Artiaga gave the writer a copy of his "Brief History of San Juan del Monte," the only available history of the town, from which the following historical account is drawn.

SAN JUAN DEL MONTE

San Juan del Monte, in the province of Rizal, is about fifteen minutes away from the heart of Manila.   The winding San Juan River is the natural and official boundary which separates it from Manila; immediately north of San Juan is Quezon City, the largest city in Rizal.   Located on top of hills overlooking Manila, San Juan benefits from a relatively cool and temperate climate, which in former days gave it a natural advantage in the control of malaria; this protection, coupled with its proximity to Manila, made it a residential favorite with person whose place of employment was in Manila (chiefly professionals and government workers).

"Old" San Juan

Although its political boundaries have changed through the years, San Juan has a long and rich history.   Its origin dates back to pre-Spanish times; San Juan's equivalent to Lycurgus or Remus and Romulus was King Lacantagean, by now a semi-legendary figure.   The Spaniards divided up the areas they conquered into huge estates, and San Juan became one of these. An early record[1] shows that in 1602 the owner of that estate gave a part of it to the Dominicans on which to construct a convent. Landholdings of the Church increased to such an extent that as late as 1910 all the land which comprised San Juan was actually the private property of friars, who leased it to farmers and other inhabitants. This gave the orders great wealth and influence, but also made them the object of envy and hatred.

Until 1783 San Juan was politically attached to the town of Santa Ana; in that year it was granted its own civil government. Nevertheless, in religious matters it continued to be a part of the parish of Santa Ana and it was not until 1892 that it acquired its own parish, under the control of Franciscan fathers. The early civil government which it had was typical of town governments throughout the Philippines. This was later replaced by a type of municipal government which gave it greater autonomy from provincial officials. During the Spanish regime the town officers were the *gobernadorcillo* or chief officer, three lieutenants, the police, and lastly the *cabezas de barangay* (perhaps best rendered in English by "village headmen"). The common people had no direct voice in choosing the above: the gobernadorcillo and his lieutenants were selected by ex-*gobernadorcillos* and *cabezas de barangay* with the elections supervised by the Civil Governor of the province.[2] It must also be noted that during the Spanish colonial period great power was wielded in the community by the sacerdotal office, due to the union of Church and State.

In the 1890s political unrest and dissatisfaction with the Spanish regime began to spread through the Philippines; a revolutionary society called the Katipunan was the great rallying point for those seeking independence. The head of this society, Andres Bonifacio, now a national hero, made frequent visits with his aides to San Juan and soon the great majority of able-bodied males became members of that society. A stronghold of the Katipunan, San Juan became the scene on August 30, 1896, of the first actual combat between the Spanish and the revolutionary forces. Although set back in this initial encounter, Filipino revolutionaries had managed by the time Admiral Dewey appeared on the scene two years later to restrict Spanish military activity to a small radius around Manila.

The Treaty of Paris of 1898 which ceded, among other things, the Philippines to the United States was a bitter pill to swallow for the Filipinos, who had expected that the expulsion of the Spaniards would result in immediate independence. Instead of independence, they found their country occupied by another foreign power. The uneasy tensions between the American army and the Filipino forces came to a head on February 4, 1899, with the exchange of shots between the Filipino and American sentry at opposite ends of the San Juan bridge, right in San Juan del Monte. This actually launched the war between the two armies, and unknown to most Americans, the second Filipino War of Independence continued until 1901, when all the insurgents were finally put down. Thus we can see that San Juan was actively involved in its nation's historical development.

Few demographic facts are available concerning San Juan prior to the American occupation, although its population in the 1890s probably stood at about 2,500 inhabitants, according to various reports submitted by the "village headmen" to the parish priest. The ravages of the fighting during the War of 1898 led to a sharp population decrease, due to the exodus of many inhabitants for safer parts. Soon after peace and order were restored, an influx of persons from surrounding communities offset this decrease, and San Juan's population has been steadily rising until today (1956) it numbers more than 35,000 inhabitants, according to municipal estimates.

In the old days (pre-American) San Juan was sparsely populated; much of the land was devoted to growing rice and, to a secondary extent, sugar cane. A few Chinese-owned sari-sari stores sold to the inhabitants whatever commodities could not be grown on the land. The town's industry was limited to a rope factory, the largest at that time in the Philippines, and to a small soap factory. At the turn of the century San Juan became an important center for the making of *carretalas*, small horse carriages still in evidence today. To complete the picture, San Juan boasted a public school, a church, and a building which became during the hot season the temporary residence of the Spanish Governor General of the Philippines.

Briefly, one can say that San Juan before the present century was essentially an agricultural community, with secondary importance as a residential area for government officials and others working in Manila.

San Juan Today[3]

San Juan has had a rapid growth in the last fifty years: the 1948 Census placed its population at 31,493,[4] which represents an increase of 472 per cent over the figure for 1918; during the same period the Province of Rizal had a population growth of 192 per cent. This rate of growth seems characteristic of underdeveloped areas with a high growth potential and is in the main attributable to the slashing down of the death rate with a relative constancy in the crude birth rate. For the period January-September 1954, San Juan had an average crude birth rate of 34.2 per thousand while its crude death rate was only 7.6, leaving an excess of 26.6 per thousand.[5] Thus, we can say that San Juan's growth is a reflection of both natural increase and in-migration. Out of 29 municipalities in Rizal, San Juan ranks seventh in size.

In 1948 its population was divided into 5,623 families for an average of about 5.5 members per household. The sex ratio shows a slight excess of females (52 per cent). The age distribution reveals that the population of San Juan is essentially a young one: 50 per cent being under 20 years of age, 40 per cent being in the age bracket 20-44, and only 10 per cent reported as being over 44 years of age.[6]

Culturally, San Juan is a predominant Tagalog-Catholic community. Nearly 100 per cent are reported able to speak Tagalog with 63 and 12 per cent able to speak English and Spanish respectively.[7] In religious conviction, 94 per cent classify themselves as Roman Catholics (the provincial average is 88 per cent), two per cent each are Protestants and Aglipayans, one per cent belongs to the Iglesia ni Kristo (Church of Christ)[8] and the remainder forms a residual category of non-believers or adherents to Buddhism.[9]

Ethnically, the population is broken into five racial categories recognized by the Bureau of the Census: Brown, Yellow, White, Black, and Mixed.[10] Out of 31,493 inhabitants in the last census, 30,085 or 95 per cent of the population of San Juan were part of the Brown race; the remaining five per cent was taken up by members of the Yellow race (chiefly Chinese), Whites (Americans and Europeans), and Mixed, with only three inhabitants of San Juan classified as Black.[11] For the whole of Rizal Province the 1948 data indicate that out of a total population of over 670,000 there were about 666,000 individuals (99 per cent) classified as belonging to the Brown race, with most of the residual one per cent classified in the Yellow race.   Thus, while San Juan inhabitants are overwhelmingly Malayan in racial origin (and within this group the Tagalog element is in the majority), it has a somewhat higher percentage of persons not classified in the Brown race than other urban centers, especially those further away from Manila.   In this respect, San Juan is somewhat more "cosmopolitan" than other areas.

San Juan has the highest literacy rate in Rizal, and certainly one of the highest in the Philippines.   Eighty-six per cent of those fifteen years and over are able to read and write (92 per cent of the males and 81 per cent of the females), while the average of Rizal province as a whole is 77 per cent (83 per cent of the males, 72 per cent of the females).[12]   As might be expected, literacy rates show a marked age differential: in the age group 20-24 years 90 per cent of the males and 83 per cent of the females are able to read and write, but this percentage steadily declines in the higher age categories so that for the ge group consisting of those 65 years and older only 43 and 24 per cent of males and females respectively are reported to be literate.[13]   This great contrast sharply reflects a basic difference between the Spanish and the American administrations: the Spaniards greatly hindered the spread of public education on a mass basis whereas the Americans did as much as possible to make it possible.   Considering how long the Spaniards occupied the Philippines in comparison to the American reign, a visitor to the Philippines is amazed at the extent to which the use of English is so widespread and conversely the extent to which Spanish is spoken by only a small minority; one factor making for this situation is that the Spaniards did not encourage the Filipinos to learn Spanish whereas the Americans made English a subject taught in all the public schools.[14]

Economically, San Juan today is no longer a predominantly agricultural community but presents rather a healthy, diversified economy.   How many of its inhabitants are employed in the community in comparison to being employed outside of San Juan (especially Manila) is not known to any degree of accuracy, but the latter must form a sizeable group.   In estimated yearly income received from all sources (for the population), San Juan ranks fifth in the province out of 29 municipalities: it ranks third in such sources as government, personal services, professional services, mining and quarrying, and agriculture (including forestry, hunting and fishing); it ranks fifth in sources from recreation, sixth in manufacturing, transportation and communication, and commerce, and finally, it ranks eighth in construction.[15] Although the detailed breakdown of gainfully employed workers by specific occupational groups is lacking, the aforementioned figures suggest that a high percentage are employed in public service, such as government employees, in the professions, and in skilled and semi-skilled occupations.

In household commodities San Juan is also well ahead of the provincial average, which, in turn, is well ahead of the national average. For example, 23 per cent of the families in San Juan live in houses built of strong materials (reinforced concrete, concrete and structural steel, etc.) compared to only nine per cent for the whole of Rizal; 79 per cent of the families in San Juan use electricity for lighting against 65 per cent for the whole province; also, 26 per cent have radios against the provincial average of 19 per cent.[16]

Over the years the municipal budget has steadily risen until today it stands above 500,000 pesos (officially $250,000), which is quite large for a Filipino municipality of this size. The major source of revenues comes from rentals of the public market stalls, which is a big center of attraction. Collections from realty taxes is an important secondary source which accounts for almost a third of the income. Several industries have been attracted to San Juan because there is no taxation on new industries for the first ten years: for example, the largest maker of radios and electronic appliances in the Philippines has developed its factory in San Juan. San Juan also has several biscuit factories, a soap-making factory, a toy-making factory, and a meat packing plant.

San Juan del Monte, although on the whole a prosperous and growing community, does present sharp contrasts in standards of living, and in physical appearances. It has very wealthy residents living in large sumptuous homes, but it also has its slum areas, bordering chiefly along the banks of the San Juan River. Some of its inhabitants have to live in flimsy "barong-barong" or squatters' huts, which are makeshift constructions having no windows and no sanitary facilities. Most of the streets are not paved and do not have electric lights at night to illuminate them.

San Juan, then, seemed to be a suitable location from which to draw an urban sample. On the whole it is economically better off than most urban communities, and certainly it is more exposed to the influences of Manila, due to its spatial proximity to this teeming metropolis. Nevertheless, its socio-cultural ethos is fairly representative of Tagalog urban centers, but we do not mean to claim that it is "the" typical urban community. Moreover, San Juan presents the advantage of having a long history and actual close contacts with both Spanish and American cultural orientations, which was a desideratum in the selection of the urban sample.

RURAL AREAS

In the selection of the rural areas, it was thought that the following criteria would be useful: a) the localities chosen should be at varying distances from Manila and other urban centers, b) the localities should be on the whole Tagalog-speaking, so as to hold at least one element of "culture" constant, but one community should be non-Tagalog for contrast and c) the areas should be as representative as possible of rural-agricultural Central Luzon. The writer had numerous conferences with the personnel of the U.S. Foreign Operations Mission in the Philippines, with the Philippines Rural Reconstruction Movement, and with staff members of the Department of Sociology and Social Welfare of the University of the Philippines. These conversations were of immense help in deciding what sort of communities should be sought, but the choice of particular sites was the writer's own. It is difficult for an external observer to decide what constitutes the rural Filipino "Jonesville," but nevertheless, impressionistic observations seem to warrant the assumption that the final rural sample of this project is to a large extent representative of the Central Luzon population.

Nangka[17]

The first rural area selected was barrio Nangka, politically a unit of the town of Marikina, in the province of Rizal. Nangka is located about four miles north of the poblacion of Marikina; it is the same distance away from Quezon City, the future capital of the Philippines, and only 13 miles away from Manila. Easy access to these three is made possible by an asphalt road which traverses the middle of Nangka and over which buses travel to Marikina for their shopping, and for recreation and amusement such as movies, cockfights, and ball games; as many as 40 per cent of the families go to see movies in Manila or Marikina, some as frequently as twice a week. Since there is only one midwife in the community, in case of a serious illness, a doctor must be called in from Marikina. All in all, Nangka inhabitants have a relatively high degree of familiarity with urban centers.

Geographically, Nangka is situated in the Marikina valley, surrounded on both sides by hills in the distance; to the west runs the Marikina River and to the east the Nangka River, which flows into the former shortly north of the barrio. Surrounding and interpenetrating Nangka are rice fields, which are cultivated without means of modern mechanization, but by the time-honored system of one-man-one-water buffalo-one-iron plow. The area cultivated by each farmer is very small, averaging about three hectares only.

Of Nangka's 188 families (representing slightly over 1,000 persons, for an average of about 5.5 members per household), only 60 or less than a third are engaged in farming; 58 of these 60 families do not own the land they cultivate but work for absentee landowners, thus giving Nangka one of the highest rates of farm tenancy in the Philippines, the national average being placed at about 35 per cent, and the average for Central Luzon at 60 per cent in 1948.

The distribution of heads of households shows that after farming, the largest percentage is occupied as unskilled workers (sand and gravel diggers, laborers) representing 24 per cent of the families. Next are skilled workers (primarily shoemakers mostly working in Marikina) who represent another 21 per cent of all the families. The remainder are engaged as storekeepers, unskilled workers, and miscellaneous or unemployed. Only one professional, a civil engineer, resides in Nangka, but his place of employment is in Manila.

Economically, semi-skilled workers have the highest average income, about $70 per month (computed on the official rate of exchange: two Filipino pesos = one U.S. dollar), followed by storekeepers and skilled workers, who average between $50-$55 a month; unskilled workers earn somewhat less than $45, and those engaged in farming average only about $35 a month, but even this modest sum is higher than the average for farmers in Central Luzon.

Nangka has been selected by the national Philippine Rural Reconstruction Movement as a model *barrio*, one in which modern methods of soil fertilization, home industries such as handloom weaving, fish culture to supplement the staple of rice, and other innovations designed to improve the standard of living will be and have been introduced. But this project is quite recent and the path to improvement arduous. Ninety per cent of the houses still lack sanitary facilities; over a fifth of the families obtain their water supply from the Marikina River and open wells; the unbalanced diet produced a high rate of beriberi and skin diseases, while malaria, diarrhea and tuberculosis are nor uncommon. Education facilities are limited to one schoolhouse (built in 1949) which provides for only the first two grades of primary education, and illiteracy is still an acute problem. Only one family owns a radio set. Finally it may be mentioned that unemployment and under-employment are prevalent, especially in the age group 14-34. In spite of this, post-World War II population increase has been high, due to in-migration as well as natural increase; the strength of family ties is a strong factor in discouraging emigration to other areas.

Nangka, in summary, presents many of the features and problems of rural Filipino areas. But in contrast to many, it has a high degree of community cohesion, and with the present help of the PRRM, it should greatly improve its material status.

Santo Tomas (Lubao)

Barrio Santo Tomas belongs to the municipality of Lubao, in the province of Pampanga, which is northwest of Manila. The 85 kilometers which separate it from Manila (a little over 50 miles) require about two and a half hours, making allowance for bus connections, the most important means of transportation. To reach Santo Tomas one leaves Manila by bus (loaded with passengers, vegetables, firewood, and live poultry) and heads north through the province of Bulacan, passing through the rich farming valley of

Central Luzon which bestows wealth to absentee landlords residing in Manila and arduous toil to the hard-working farm tenants. The road leads to San Fernando, provincial capital of Pampanga, 17 kilometers (about 10 miles) away from Santo Tomas. Since buses from Manila do not as a rule discharge passengers in small villages such as Santo Tomas, one has to change at the city of Guagua and from there take a jeepney (a World War II jeep converted for passenger use and often having as many as ten or more riders) to San Tomas, about fifteen minutes away. Along the paved road one sees on either side dense vegetation of mango orchards, bamboo trees, and the like, alternating with great flat patches of rice fields. The countryside tends to be very flat, but the road is very winding.

Santo Tomas lies on either side of the road coming from Guagua and going to the adjacent *población* or municipality of Lubao, one and a half kilometers away. For their sustenance the people raise rice, corn, and camote (related to the sweet potato); in addition to some chickens and pigs (the latter eaten only during fiestas or special celebrations), their diet is supplemented with a profusion of mangoes, bananas, and guavas, all of which grow very easily.

This is not a Tagalog-speaking area; the language spoken is called Kapampango (or Pampango for short). Tagalog and Kapampango are quite distinct from one another, as much as French and English. The language distinction is perhaps the most salient difference between Santo Tomas and Tagalog rural communities, at least to a foreign observer. Dwellings in both have the same form, being built out of bamboo and nipa palms; physical appearance of both inhabitants is strikingly similar, and Roman Catholicism is the dominant religious belief system in both communities (about 90 per cent of the inhabitants of Central Luzon are Catholics).

Accurate statistical information concerning various aspects of social life in Santo Tomas is lacking, but the great majority of the population is engaged in farming, and especially in rice cultivation, with the overwhelming majority being tenants. Some find employment as workers in the sugar centrals (where the cane is refined) located in San Fernando, and a few of the inhabitants even go to Manila to find work as stevedores and other unskilled jobs.

At present Santo Tomas is a peaceful *barrio*, but about five years or so ago it felt the dissident activities of the Communist-supported Huk guerrillas who terrorized Central Luzon. There are no schools in Santo Tomas; the inhabitants send their children to the one elementary school in nearby Lubao. There is one Roman Catholic chapel but it has no permanent parish priest. There are three teachers, one physician, and one midwife, who can be said to constitute the professional elite of Santo Tomas. For recreation such as movies the inhabitants go to Guagua or on special occasions to San Fernando; however, cockfighting, dances and fiestas are still the most widespread form of local entertainment. Any stranger coming to Santo Tomas is the object of great curiosity, around which gather the men not immediately working in the rice fields and all the available women and children; all Americans are called "Joe" in fond remembrance of the American G.I.s who fought the Japanese over much of this terrain.

Amacalan (Gerona)

Barrio Amacalan is located on the paved highway that connects Tarlac, capital of the province of Tarlac, with Gerona, the municipality to which Amacalan is politically attached. The total population of Gerona and its constituent parts was estimated by the local 1953 census to be 28,542; Amacalan's population in 1954 was slightly more than 900, of which a third was under 10 years of age.

Amacalan is four kilometers south of Gerona and about 15 kilometers north of the city of Tarlac. Access to both is usually by means of jeepneys and small open-air buses which run at frequent intervals. To the east of Amacalan are the tracks of the Manila Railroad which cuts through Central Luzon. The paved road which bisects Amacalan is actually a part of the national highway which connects Manila (135 kilometers away) with the mountainous summer resort of Baguio, further to the north.

Unlike the other rural communities of this study, the most important part of soil cultivation in Amacalan is devoted not to rice but to the growing of sugar cane; three wealthy families own most of the land in this barrio, including the cane fields. Ninety per cent of all farmers are tenants and are officially supposed to keep 70 per cent of the harvest, the remainder going to the landlord (this share system varies in Central Luzon but very often, either with or without government sanction, the landlord gets a full half).

One crop of palay (unpolished rice) is raised a year, without benefit of irrigation. Crop rotation is followed and after the palay harvest the farm tenants raise vegetables, peanuts, camote, as well as extensive planting of sugar cane. Most of the male adults become workers in the sugar cane fields after the all-important rice harvest is in.

One third of the population is composed of children under ten years of age. At present about 200 children 6-13 years of age are attending the elementary school, which is the most prominent building in Amacalan; the six teachers and the principal of the school are the only professionals in the barrio. Sixteen per cent of the males and 26 per cent of the females ten years old and over are illiterate, for a combined average of 20 per cent, which is lower than the average of 29 per cent found in the study of Rivers and McMillan of barrios in Central Luzon.[18]

Of Amacalan's 141 families, 28 per cent are equipped with toilets in their home, 69 per cent keep pigs and/or poultry, and 18 per cent receive some newspapers or magazines, mostly written in the local dialects of Tagalog and Ilocano. One hundred families are Roman Catholics, twenty belong to the native Church of Christ (Iglesia ni Kristo), five to the independent Aglipayan, ten families are Seventh Day Adventists, and five are Protestants.

For those who can afford to continue beyond the six years of elementary school, high school facilities are found in Tarlac, and a private high school is in Gerona. For post-secondary education, the privileged few go to college in Manila.

The average number of household members is 6.5, and the population increase of 35 per cent between 1948 and 1954 is due to natural increase, chiefly the result of cutting down the death rate by means of sanitary measures. As in many other communities in Central Luzon, Amacalan will soon have to face the problem of over-population, due to population increase and the relatively small amount of land available for farming. The dependency of the barrio on sugar cane fields for its source of employment, aside from farming, leaves it economically vulnerable, but for the present its inhabitants lead a rather contented life.

La Paz

The last rural community selected is actually not one entity, but three separate barrios clustered around the *poblacion* of La Paz, which, with a population placed in the 1948 Census at just under 20,000, ranks seventh in size out of 17 municipalities in the province of Tarlac. La Paz is connected to Tarlac City, about 25 kilometers to the northwest, by means of various rough dirt roads that present no serious obstacle to the windowless buses which, racing at breakneck speed, suck in great quantities of dirt and coat the passengers with a solid layer from head to toes.

The three barrios selected (Macalong, San Isidro and San Roque) have a combined population of nearly 4,000 inhabitants,most of whom speak Tagalog, but in the whole of the municipality Ilocano is also widely spoken. The average number of members per household is reported to be about 7.5, which makes it the highest average in our sample.

Two of the barrios are actually within the municipal boundary of La Paz and the third, Macalong, is four and a half kilometers to the north.

A short distance away from the *poblacion*, to the east of La Paz, is the large Rio Chico river, which marks the boundary between the provinces of Tarlac and Nueva Ecija. During 1949-50 much of this area was the scene of some of the most bitter agrarian uprisings in the whole of Central Luzon, but today the greater part of the dissident activity has subsided. Farming is the chief occupation; the rich soil and the availability of water for irrigation help to make La Paz the rice granary of Tarlac province. The river makes fishing also a worthwhile mode of occupation. As was the case in the other rural ares in the sample, tenancy rates are very high, about 85 per cent not owning the land on which they live and toil. Absentee landlords, living in Manila or other places, come once a year during harvest time to collect their share.

La Paz boasts a city hall which has a post office, one elementary school which provides for the first six years of education, and one private high school, owned by an ex-mayor. There are four churches in La Paz: Methodist, Church of Christ (Iglesia ni Kristo), Aglipayan, and of course, a Roman Catholic one. Next to the city hall is a farmer's cooperative marketing association and around the *poblacion* one can find a tailor, a grocery store, several sari-sari stores (a small-size hybrid between a grocery store, a drug store, and a delicatessen store), and even a medical clinic run by a visiting physician. In addition there is a public market held three times a week, which attracts villagers from outlying barrios.

Although it has a respectable rank in population size in the province, La Paz does not have an "urban" atmosphere. The streets are unpaved, buildings are small and not densely placed together; there are no movies in the town (at least when the writer was there) and recreation must be sought either at the cockpits or in Tarlac City, half an hour away.

* * * * * * *

The four rural communities selected in this study are not immune from contacts with urban life, but the great majority of the inhabitants still are employed in agriculture and have their deep-seated ties in a rural ethos. All the areas chosen have a very high rate of farm tenancy, which has been on the rise in Central Luzon: in 1948 about 60 per cent of all farms in Central Luzon were operated by tenants and by 1954 this had risen to 82.5 per cent; throughout the Philippines, in the same period, farm tenancy rose from 37 per cent to 53.5 per cent.[19] In our sample, at least 90-95 per cent of those engaged in farming did not own their land. Most of the areas visited either have witnessed a sharp increase in population or have a high growth potential. The further the rural area is from Manila, the less it shows signs of modernization and urban traits of life, but the gravitational attraction of the big cosmopolitan center makes itself felt in all parts of Central Luzon, and none of our communities is completely free from it.[20] Nevertheless, the contrast between our rural and urban areas is very great as far as modes of employment, social organization, and "style of life." For practical purposes, then, we can consider San Juan and our agrarian sites as tending to opposite poles of the rural-urban dichotomy, but neither represent extreme cases of this pole.

NOTES

1. Manuscripts of the Dominican Fathers in the Philippines, v. 481, cited in Artiaga, "A Brief History of San Juan," p. 1.

2. The prescribed number of electors was twelve.

3. Unless otherwise noted, all statistical and demographic information in this section was made available to the writer by the Philippine Bureau of Printing and is taken from the manuscript of the *1948 Census, Rizal Province*, which was not yet published at the time the writer was conducting his field work. The writer would like to acknowledge his gratitude to Mr. Julian Zarate of the Philippine Bureau of Printing for making available this manuscript, which will hereafter be referred to as the *1948 Census*.

4. *1948 Census* (Rizal Province), Philippine Bureau of the Census and Statistics, table 2.

5. *Monthly Health Report* (San Juan, Rizal, Bureau of Health), courtesy of Dr. Alexander Santos, Health Director.

6. *1948 Census*, table 3.

7. *Ibid.*, table 6. Some caution must be entertained as to the extent of the English spoken, since the criteria are not defined.

8. The independent sect called Iglesia ni Kristo represents a very interesting Filipino religious movement. Its founder is Felix Y. Manalo, who had an early Protestant background, but finally established his own church in 1914. Under his charismatic leadership, its members have won an increasing number of converts in recent years, although in size it is still much smaller than the

Roman Catholic or Aglipayan faiths. However, although no exact figures are available, the *per capita* wealth of its members is much greater than that of the other two faiths; many of its members are recruited from middle-class commercial interests. Its headquarters are right in San Juan, where it has a very impressive cathedral, partly built of imported Italian marble, which dominates the surroundings.

9. *Ibid.*, table 10.

10. Cf. *supra*, 29 for a brief description of these categories. For more detailed information as to the classification of racial groups see *The 1948 Census of the Philippines*, vol. I, part 1 (Manila: Bureau of the Census and Statistics, 1954), p. viii.

11. *1948 Census*, table 4.

12. *Ibid., table 16.*

13. *Ibid.*, table 15. The Census does not state explicitly the criteria for literacy; however, the writer was informed that being able to sign one's name and reading a simple paragraph are the essentials.

14. Cf. *supra*, 27.

15. *Ibid.*, table 25.

16. *Ibid.*, table 35.

17. The writer is greatly indebted to the Philippine Rural Reconstruction Movement, and especially to Mrs. Josefina Corral, Mrs. Hilaris Uy, and Mr. Teofilo Espeso, Jr., for their admirable cooperation, and for making available "A Survey of Barrio Nangka" (Philippine Rural Reconstruction Movement, 1954) from which most of the following data concerning Nangka are taken.

18. Rivera and McMillan, *The Rural Philippines*, p. 202.

19.   The inhabitants of our localities bear out the observation of Robert Redfield that " . . . he [the peasant] is long used to the existence of the city, and its ways are, in altered form, part of his ways. The peasant is a rural native whose long established order of life takes important account of the city." (*The Primitive World and Its Transformations*, Cornell University Press, 1953, p. 31.)

20.   How much this phenomenon is found in other parts of the Far East may be seen in Norton S. Ginsburg, "The Great City in Southeast Asia," *American Journal of Sociology*, LX (5): 455-462.

CHAPTER III

METHODOLOGY

The purpose of the present section is not only to describe the actual procedures used in this study, but also to discuss the difficulties and complexities of conducting a fairly large-scale sociological study in an underdeveloped area. Many of these difficulties will appear strikingly familiar to anthropologists who have done field work where angels and sociologists fear to tread. Just as anthropologists have increasingly in recent years discovered the richness of material in studying modern complex industrial societies, so shall sociology discover or re-discover new perspectives in looking at so-called primitive societies and areas of social and cultural transition.

A sociologist in the United States who wishes to obtain information on the evaluation of occupational roles, an evaluation which will be representative of his sampling universe, has relatively clear-cut and well-paved paths to follow. He will obtain a stratified or probability sample of his universe, the sampling of which is facilitated by census tracts, accurate census figures, and the like. He will draw from a relatively large body of personnel trained in the art of interviewing, distribute his schedules to his co-workers, and await in his office the return of filled forms. Undoubtedly this is a somewhat oversimplified and perhaps idealized exposition of the situation, but it does have resemblance to reality. To obtain similar results in an underdeveloped area such as the Philippines involves a great deal of arduous toil and manifold uncertainties as to the confidence limits of the reliability of the data. We shall attempt to describe the procedures and difficulties encountered in the urban and rural areas respectively, pointing out the similarities and differences of each.

The initial problems focused on the drawing up of a suitable questionnaire and on finding personnel which could administer them. In the formulation of the schedule, the linguistic problem loomed large. The writer had been assured that Filipinos in or about Manila were nearly as proficient in speaking and understanding English as their own maternal tongue. The veracity of this statement is, however, related to the socio-economic status of the individual; the lower a Filipino's social position, the less, *on the average*, is his ability to comprehend and express himself in English. When this became apparent, it was considered necessary that the questionnaire should be administered in either English or Tagalog, the language predominantly spoken in and about Manila, including, naturally, San Juan del Monte.

Accordingly, the English form was translated into Tagalog by a professional translator, who was instructed to render it into everyday idiomatic speech, rather than formal literary translation. In constructing the original form in English the writer attempted to avoid phrases and expressions which might be considered "culture-bound," but this is not to claim that he was completely successful in this endeavor. The Tagalog translation was given to persons of varying socio-economic status and educational achievement whose maternal tongue was Tagalog. They were asked (individually) to translate or phrase to the writer the questions into English, and to state what they understood the questions to mean. The writer was thus able to compare their translation with the original English form.   Since the responses showed great similarities in the translations, and since there was a marked congruence between what the writer intended the questions to mean and what the respondents understood the questions to mean, it was thought possible to retain the original translated Tagalog form and incorporate it in the schedule.[1]

Because the writer had no prior familiarity with Tagalog, the task of conducting several hundred interviews in the short period of time at his disposal would have been almost insurmountable. It was therefore apparent that native interviewers should conduct the actual administration of the schedules, not only for linguistic purposes, but also because of another basic reason. In a sense, the Philippines has only recently emerged from a period of colonialism, in which there was (and to a large extent still is) a marked inegalitarian relationship between Filipinos on the one hand and Europeans and Americans on the other. What struck the writer was how frequently a Filipino tells an American not what he thinks, but what he thinks the American wants to hear. Along with this is the unconscious fear that ignorance of an answer to a question will cause a "loss of face." In other words, it was the impression of the writer that it would be very difficult for a Filipino in an interview situation with an American to "be himself," and to express the same opinions that he would to his neighbor. Moreover, as was well demonstrated in the rural areas, an American coming to the home of a Filipino to conduct an interview would be the object of great curiosity on the part of all household members and even neighbors, so that the interview situation would be greatly complicated. For these reasons, it was decided to rely on native Filipinos.

To find persons familiar with techniques of interviewing presented another problem. It seemed that on the whole college students who were bi-lingual in Tagalog and English would be acceptable, in the face of the scarcity of adult interviewers with previous experience. Through the kind help of the Department of Sociology and Social Welfare at the University of Manila, and especially of Professor John de Young who as Director of the Social Science Research Center had already conducted some sociological surveys in the Philippines, the writer was able to contact about half a dozen college students with some experience at interviewing. About 20 additional students showed interest in the project, and one long training session was devoted to familiarize them with the proper ways of conducting an interview.

The meaning of each question in the schedule was carefully explained, and the students were instructed to turn in at the field offices the respondents' answers in English, although during the interview itself the responses could be written down in Tagalog. When the questionnaires were brought in during the actual survey, the writer's assistant^2 checked all responses to make certain the students' translations were adequate and as accurate as possible. However, it must be admitted that if the interviewer only turned in responses in English, without giving the original Tagalog, we had no way of checking on the accuracy of the translation.   We had informed the interviewers that if they were not sure how to translate certain responses, they should just submit the spontaneous Tagalog answers of the respondent; in such cases the translation was done at the field office.

During the training session, the writer and his assistant conducted a practice interview in front of the students. Furthermore, each student was told to conduct two practice interviews with persons in their neighborhood other than family members; these schedules were brought to the writer and his assistant and each questionnaire was carefully gone over with the interviewer.   These interviews formed the pre-test and an analysis of these interviews showed that no major change was needed in the construction of the questionnaire.   Furthermore, it revealed that college students were quite capable of conducting the interviews and obtaining the data sought.

Prior to the actual interviewing in San Juan the problem of sampling had to be confronted.   In setting up a stratified sample one must know the characteristics of the population such as age, income, education, occupation, etc.   Post-war census data were not then available, and it was not until the survey had already been underway that the Bureau of Printing made available parts of the manuscript of the 1948 Census.   Census tracts are not used, neither does the municipality of San Juan keep a police list of its inhabitants, so that getting a probability sample would have been very difficult and time-consuming, especially since this would have required an enumeration of all the dwelling units.   What suggested itself was, under the circumstances, a form of quota sampling.   From the Philippine Electoral Commission in Manila the writer was able to obtain a complete listing of the electoral districts of San Juan; the geographical demarcation of each district was also provided so that each interviewer could be assigned to a given territory.   From the total list of 85 electoral precincts, 35 precincts were selected by means of a table of random numbers, which gave a sampling ratio of about four out of ten.   The chosen precincts were shown to municipal authorities who gave assurance that these gave a representative cross-section of San Juan, in terms of the socio-economic status of the inhabitants. The interviewers assigned to a particular precinct were told to complete twenty schedules each. They were told to familiarize themselves with their own precinct, and to get as equal a number as possible of respondents living in what would be considered in such an urban community as above-average, average and below-average homes. On each schedule the interviewer was told to rate separately the external and internal appearances of the dwelling.[3] This procedure is a loose form of quota sampling and not beyond reproach by any means, but other alternatives seemed too costly and time-consuming. Interviewers were to administer only one schedule per household, and to interview a person who was or had been gainfully employed, preferably the household head. This qualification of past or previous employment was to ensure the respondent's familiarity with the occupational structure, but it does restrict our sample to members of the labor force. In this sense, then, we cannot claim that our sample is representative of the total population.

A further problem of doing a public opinion poll in the Philippines was anticipated. In the United States, based on the experiences of the writer, the respondent's initial suspicion of a pollster or interviewer is that he is really a salesman in disguise who will attempt to make the respondent buy a magazine subscription, kitchen utensils, and the like. In the Philippines the initial suspicion is that the interviewer is a government employee; several Filipinos mentioned to the writer that census takers or government employees passing as census takers had found out a great deal about personal income and wealth, with the result that a short time after the interview surprised individuals found their personal taxes suddenly increased. Thus every care was taken in this study to inform respondents that interviewers were not government employees but college students from the University of the Philippines engaged in a public opinion study of people's attitudes toward occupations. The interviewers were also provided with identification papers; as it turned out, very few respondents asked to have these shown. It was also pointed out to the respondents at the outset that there was absolutely no right or wrong answer to any question, that all we were interested in were his own opinions, and that other members of the family should refrain from answering any question or making comments during the course of the interview.

The questionnaire itself was designed to take about one hour in its administration.   In a sense, the most strategic part was the evaluation of given occupational roles.   The writer had chosen a final list of 30 occupations, which seemed to meet the following criteria: most of the occupations would be familiar to all respondents; the occupations should be a good cross-section of the occupational structure of the Philippines, or at least of Central Luzon; and finally, as many items as possible should be the same as or similar to occupations evaluated in previous studies.   The final list arrived at was the following (in alphabetical order):

1. barber
2. bus or jeepney driver
3. carpenter
4. congressman
5. construction worker
6. domestic servant
7. engineer
8. enlisted man, armed forces
9. factory worker
10. farm tenant
11. farmer
12. fisherman
13. gasoline station attendant
14. intermediate school teacher
15. lawyer
16. manager of business company
17. midwife
18. office clerk
19. officer in armed forces
20. owner of sari-sari store
21. physician
22. priest
23. policeman
24. produce peddlar
25. professional artist
26. road repairman
27. salesman
28. sugar plantation worker
29. tailor
30. university professor

A few words might be said as to the rationale for including some of the above occupations, which may not be familiar to non-Filipinos.

Buses and jeepneys are the most prevalent forms of land transportation in Central Luzon.   Jeepneys are for the most part surplus American jeeps used during the American occupation of 1944-45.   They have been converted into passenger vehicles which comfortably accommodate five passengers, but during rush hours it is not unusual to see as many as ten or more individuals hanging on for dear life as the jeepney dodges in and out of traffic; jeepney drivers, like bus drivers, do not for the great majority own their vehicle.   A great many bus and jeepney drivers carry in front of them an image of a Catholic Saint or of the Holy Family with a sign reading "God be with us."   The latter attests not only their religious belief, but also the need of some good-luck piece to carry them safely through the hazardous driving conditions (no speed limits, few policemen, and a great scarcity of traffic lights--by and large, driving around Manila comes very close to a Hobbesian state of "war of all against all"). Since jeepneys in the outlying regions are the most frequently used vehicles connecting adjacent barrios, and buses the most used form of traveling from one town or city to another, it was thought that these occupations would be quite familiar to both urban and rural respondents.

Sari-sari stores are small, independently owned retail stores which are found throughout the Philippines. Cookies, canned goods, soft drinks and a host of household commodities can be purchased at these stores, which are somewhat equivalent to an old-fashioned American general store. Since it takes relatively little capital to operate one, this occupation is representative or typical of those who are self-employed shopkeepers,

Produce peddlers are very common in urban areas, and to some extent in rural areas. They go from house to house shouting their specialties as they pass along; some will sell coconuts, others cheese, rice cakes, ducks' eggs, etc. They also tend to be self-employed, but their margin of profit is very low in comparison to other small businessmen, and their chances of improving their status is equally low. Produce peddlers are increasingly becoming remnants of a previous age, but as long as the standard of living remains low and modern methods of food marketing are limited in their application, these individuals continue to be familiar figures.

Limiting the list to 30 occupations had one pragmatic basis. It was felt by the writer that a much greater number would give respondents difficulties in rating one occupation in relation to all other occupations. Of course, one way of avoiding this difficulty, as was used by the National Opinion Research Center in their national survey of the evaluation of occupations in the United States, is to have the respondents place the occupation on a given scale, without consideration to other occupations presented; another more laborious procedure is that of paired comparison. However, it remains to be shown which method has greater validity, regardless of computational elegance. It must be admitted that the method of ranking used does not reveal the respondent's *intensity* in the way he evaluates one occupation relative to another (that is, there may objectively be a rank difference of one between an occupation placed first and the one ranked second but for the respondent this may signify a world of difference). However, it must be noted that the method of the NORC survey did not find out how intensively the respondent felt about evaluating a given occupation in relation to the other occupations presented.

A very important procedural consideration in asking respondents to evaluate occupational roles is the frame of reference in which such judgments are to be made. Unfortunately, the literature does not show any standardization in the instructions given to the respondents, or in some studies the wording of the instructions is left out. The NORC instructed their respondents as follows: "For each job mentioned, please pick out the statement that best gives *your own personal opinion* of the *general standing* that such a job has." Then followed these alternatives:

1. Excellent standing
2. Good standing
3. Average standing
4. Somewhat below average standing
5. Poor standing
6. I don't know where to place that one[4]

In our study urban respondents were presented with a set of 30 3x5 cards; on the front of each card the occupational title was written in Tagalog, on the back the Spanish and English equivalent were given. The instructions (appropriately translated in Tagalog) read:

> We have here some cards, each of which has an occupation written on it. If you think these occupations are of different social standing (do not have the same social evaluation, do not have the same social rank, do not have the same prestige), please arrange them in order of decreasing social standing with the highest rated occupation on top, then the next highest, and so on. Place together those occupations that you cannot arrange in this sort of order. Please remember that there is no correct way to do this arranging and that we are only interested in *your* judgment.

This procedure which is in the main similar to that used by the NORC is open to the following criticism, which must be frankly acknowledged. By asking the respondent to give his own opinion or judgment of the social standing of a given occupation, are we finding out what the   respondent perceives to be the social consensus, what he personally considers the evaluation to be, or a mixture of both? Phrased differently, are we obtaining an objective evaluation or a subjective one or a combination of both? Does the respondent have as a frame of reference the consensus of the country, of the community in which he lives, or of the socio-economic stratum to which he belongs (or possibly, his reference group which may or may not coincide with his actual position)? In raising these questions, we may be opening Pandora's box, whose ills will vitiate some of our findings and those of previous studies of occupational stratification; but the writer agrees with the Classical Greeks that the way to wisdom is through suffering. So far, studies in this field of sociology have emphasized amazing and relatively clear-cut empirical results but have neglected to face serious methodological problems such as the above. In the future, research should be done into the significance of the results, not in more empirical findings.

In the present investigation there was an attempt to tap at the frames of reference each respondent used. In addition to having him rank the 30 occupations presented, he was also asked to state why he had ranked each of the top three and each of the bottom three occupations the way he did. Our findings will be given in a later chapter, but it can be mentioned here that not only do different respondents have different frames of reference for the prestige of a given occupation, but that the same respondent may show a plurality of reference-systems.

A few words need to be said about the procedures used in contacting respondents in rural areas. Choosing interviewers was an immediate problem, in many ways similar to an anthropologist selecting an informant who is not marginal or deviant to his community. The interviewer not only had to have intimate knowledge of his community so as to get a representative sample in a short period of time, but also be able to comprehend the scope of the survey and lastly to transcribe the answers in English (since the coding of the data was to be done in the United States).[5] The majority of interviewers finally selected were school teachers, but also included were members of the Philippine Rural Reconstruction Movement (in Nangka), municipal employees, and others. With each interviewer the writer discussed the purpose of the study, as well as every part of the schedule. Each interviewer was asked to fill a sample questionnaire for himself, and to conduct another practice interview under the supervision of the writer. After each interviewer felt at ease with the questionnaire, he was instructed to get as representative as possible a cross-section of the area to which he was assigned. In Nangka publicity for the study was given by the Philippine Rural Reconstruction Movement and by well-known and popular citizens, so that the villagers were acquainted prior to being interviewed with the aim of the study. In Santo Tomas the writer administered a questionnaire to the interviewer selected; what was meant to be a private training session turned into an informal public holiday. Dozens of villagers, including all the children, most of the women, and several stray dogs, surrounded the strange American who seemed to be giving a test to a respected teacher! After the interview, which consumed nearly three hours, the writer was allowed to dodge from the curious, but friendly, throng of children surrounding him by having a sari-sari store owner pass out free cookies to all. This, it is hoped, served to strengthen Filipino-American relations.

This incident illustrates the high visibility of a foreigner in a relatively isolated rural community, and points to the desirability of having as interviewers individuals well-known and respected to the villagers. However, it may well be the case that school teachers, for example, have a prestige which makes the respondent feel inferior and constrained in his answers, so that the interview situation has an inegalitarian dimension. Whether this, in fact, did influence the answers is only a conjecture, but this potential problem is one to be acknowledged.

In administering the questionnaire in rural areas it was anticipated that quite a large number of respondents might be illiterate, and hence could not sort a deck of cards with written stimuli. The procedure used to overcome this difficulty (rather than have the interviewer read aloud the list of occupations in alphabetical sequence) was perhaps naive, but accomplished its purpose with great ease. The writer took informal snapshots of persons engaged in as many occupations on the list as possible (these were the following: barber, bus and jeepney drivers, construction worker, enlisted man in the armed forces, gasoline station attendant, office clerk, officer in the armed forces, owner of a sari-sari store, policeman, priest, produce peddlar, and tailor). These, with the exception of armed forces personnel and priest, were taken in places of typical work situation. Pictures of persons engaged in other occupations on the list were found in newspapers, magazines, and other periodicals. A few pictures (domestic servant, congressman, lawyer, salesman, and manager of a rice mill, which was used instead of manager of a business company because rural respondents would be more familiar with the former) were drawn by a commercial artist. Copies of the same photograph or picture were clipped on a 3x6 or 4x6 card, on the back of which the occupational title was written in Tagalog, Spanish, and English. Each interviewer received a complete deck of 30 cards, which were numbered on the back in the proper alphabetical sequence to be presented.   Prior to giving out the cards to the respective interviewers, the writer had shown the deck to various Filipinos with differing socio-educational status, and the results had been highly encouraging. This pre-test showed that respondents could easily abstract from the particular individual in the picture to the occupational role represented and make rankings accordingly, rather than on the basis of psychological reaction to specific individuals. Undoubtedly this is a somewhat crude procedure which needs greater standardization, but it proved facile to administer, and interviewers reported that it added to the enjoyment of the respondents in answering the questionnaire.

The schedules used in the urban and in the rural areas were similar, except that a few questions were added in those administered in the latter; these questions dealt with matters not pertinent to the present study.   Since the rural areas showed a much greater homogeneity in such matters as standard of living, dwelling units, and forms of employment than the urban community selected, it was not thought necessary to have as large a rural sample.

The rural interviewers were instructed to take a cross-section of persons in their community, one that would be representative of the labor force.   This procedure was necessitated by financial considerations and time limitations.   The final sample contained about five times as many urban as rural respondents, but this ratio had not been predetermined in advance.

One last point may be mentioned on the administration of the ranking of the occupations selected. In all cases, the interviewers were instructed to present the stimulus cards by the alphabetical order of the occupations. This was done as a matter of expediency to facilitate the task of the interviewer. The writer felt that if each interviewer had been asked to rotate the order of presentation in several fashions this would have led to some confusion on the part of individuals who had previously never conducted interviews. The respondents were informed that the list was to be given in alphabetical sequence, and that this sequence was not to be interpreted as the objectively correct ranking. Interviewers reported no difficulty on the part of respondents in understanding this set of instructions. Furthermore, it is encouraging to note that Campbell in his study found the *smallest* rank correlation between any pair of the rankings he obtained by means of eight different orders of presentation of the occupational stimulus to be .96. His observation was that:

> On the basis of this evidence, one may conclude that the variations in the stimulus situation induced by the order of presentation did not, in general, materially influence the ranking of the occupations. . . .[6]

Finally, we might mention our classificatory system of occupational roles. The occupational structure was divided into the ten following categories:

I	professionals and semi-professionals
II	managerial, executive and officials, other than farm
III	farm owners, farm managers, and independent farmers
IV	small business owners, shopkeepers, and other self-employed persons
V	clerical and sales
VI	foremen, craftsmen, and other skilled workers
VII	machine operatives, semi-skilled workers
VIII	laborers (including farm), unskilled workers
IX	public service workers (police, fire, armed services, etc.)
X	farm tenants

Wherever applicable, occupations were placed in the various categories following the designation of the United States Bureau of the Census.[7] Such "service" occupations as barber, beautician, and domestic servant were classified as semi-skilled (group VII). Farm laborers (group VIII) are distinguished from farm tenants by being migratory rather than sedentary, in working primarily for wages, and in having no land rights of their own.

The procedures used in analyzing the data will not be discussed in this section but will become manifest in the next chapters. The purpose of the present section was to acquaint the reader with some of the problems faced in gathering data of this kind in an underdeveloped area. Actually research in the Philippines presents fewer problems than many underdeveloped areas because English is relatively widely spoken and understood, and census figures, if not always reliable or up-to-date, are nevertheless available. But for an American sociologist used to the comforts of conducting interviews in urban New England communities, the present study was a stimulating socializing experience. The problems encountered gave the writer a closer feeling of empathy with his anthropological confreres who assiduously toil in areas free of census tracts and other such sociological artifacts.

NOTES

1. A separate form for Spanish-speaking respondent was not made for reasons of economy and also because these persons are almost without exception bi-lingual; the great majority can speak Tagalog as fluently as Spanish, and a great many can readily converse in English.

2. Mr. Ramon Liwanag, of the Social Science Research Center. He was of inestimable help in supervising interviews, coordinating the efforts of the interviewers, and in countless other ways. Without his aid this study would have been greatly retarded.

3. The rating was to be in terms of six explicitly differentiated categories: excellent, very good, good, average, poor, and very poor.

4. National Opinion on Occupations (University of Denver, 1947)

summarizes in the article of North and Hatt, "Jobs and Occupations: A Popular Evaluation," in Wilson and Kolb, eds., *Sociological Analysis* (New York: Harcourt, Brace and Company, 1949), pp. 464-73.

5.   In Santo Tomas, a Pampango-speaking barrio, the interviews were conducted in the native dialect.   The interviewer, a school teacher living in Santo Tomas but teaching in a nearby town, spoke English fluently and transcribed the answers into English.

6.   Campbell, *op. cit.*, 107.

7.   U.S. Department of Commerce, Bureau of the Census: *Classified Index of Occupations and Industries*, and *Alphabetical Index of Occupations and Industries* (Washington: Government Printing Office, 1950).

CHAPTER IV
ASPECTS OF THE OCCUPATIONAL STRUCTURE

In the present section we shall present two sets of data: the first are some objective characteristics of the occupational structure of our sample, and the second, the subjective beliefs and opinions of our respondents--how they feel about the occupational structure rather than their actual position in it.

OBJECTIVE CHARACTERISTICS

Size of the Sample

Below is shown the total sample, arranged by locality and sex of respondents.

Locality	Males	Females	N
San Juan	448	79	527
Nangka	48	4	52
La Paz	21	1	22
Amacalan	20	1	21
Santo Tomas	19	-	19
Total	556	85	641
% of total	87	13	100

Sampling Ratio

What this ratio is will depend on the index we take. Using the 1948 census data, San Juan had a total population of 31,493 and 5,623 families. Thus, our sample for San Juan represents only about 1.7 per cent of the total population, but nearly 9.5 per cent of all families (since only one interview was conducted in each household). The 1948 Census shows that there were 19,011 persons 15 years old and over; since none of our interviewees was under 19 years of age, our sample represents about 3 per cent of all the inhabitants of San Juan 15 years and over.[1]

Nangka has a population of 1,032 divided into 188 families; our sample represents about 5 per cent of the total population and nearly 28 per cent of all the families. Amacalan has 914 inhabitants (1954 figures), of which 603 are 10 years old and above; our sample covers about 3.5 per cent of the latter. In Santo Tomas and the three barrios surveyed in La Paz the writer was unable to get official figures of the adult population, so that an estimate of the sampling ratio is difficult to establish.

Education[2]

San Juan

The sample was broken down by sex and two main age groups, those under 40 years of age and those 40 years old and over. Eleven per cent of the sample had not gone beyond an intermediate education, 28 per cent had had some or had completed a high school education, and 48 per cent had had higher educational training (college and graduate studies). The latter figure is mainly due to the large number of professionals living in San Juan. The following is the *percentage* breakdown, by age group:

	Primary or less	Intermed.	High school	Advanced	N
< 40	8%	16%	31%	45%	294
> 40	16	11	23	50	233

Rural Areas

The combined sample for the four rural communities shows that 57 per cent had not gone beyond a primary education (including 13 per cent who had never attended school), 21 per cent had had at least some intermediate education, but had not gone further, 16 per cent had gone to high school and another 6 per cent had had college training. The major difference between those under 40 years of age and those 40 years old and over was that 22 per cent of the former had had a high school education against 9 per cent of the latter, but on the other hand, the percentage of those over 40 with a college education was slightly higher than for those under 40 years.

Age

San Juan

The following is the frequency distribution for various age groups:

< 20	20-25	26-29	30-39	40-49	50-59	60+	total
2	48	77	167	132	76	25	526

Fifty-six per cent of our urban sample consisted of persons under 40 years of age; by sex, 53 per cent of the males and 70 per cent of the females were less than 40 years old. Even so, our sample is considerably older than the population of San Juan taken together, but it must be kept in mind that our respondents are primarily household heads and other gainfully employed workers.

Rural Areas

The breakdown of the rural sample into persons under 40 years of age and those over 40 shows that 53 per cent is under 40 years, which is quite similar to the urban sample. The frequency distribution is given below:

< 20	20-25	26-29	30-39	40-49	50-59	60+	total
1	12	18	29	34	13	6	113

Religion

The following gives a percentage of comparison of religious affiliation in San Juan and in the rural sample:

	San Juan	Rural areas
Roman Catholic	87.7%	81.4%
Aglipayan	4.6	8.8
Protestant	3.0	5.3
Iglesia ni Kristo	2.4	-
other	1.1	.9
none	.8	2.7
no response	.4	.9
Total	100.0%	100.0%

The 1948 Census data for San Juan show that 94 per cent of the inhabitants are Roman Catholics, so that our sample is somewhat less than the official figure; on the other hand, our sample has proportionately more Aglipayans in San Juan than indicated by the Census (4.6 versus 2.2 per cent) and also more members of Iglesia ni Kristo. The following shows the comparison between our combined sample and the official 1948 figures for the Philippines as a whole:

	Sample	Total population[3]
Roman Catholic	87%	83%
Aglipayan	5	8
Protestant	3	2
All other	5	7

Language

San Juan

The question put to respondents, both urban and rural, was, "What language do you usually speak with members of your family?" Fifty-five per cent reported Tagalog, 18 per cent mentioned Tagalog and English, 2 per cent said only English, and but one per cent only Spanish; 17 per cent spoke two or more languages at home (not including Tagalog and English or Tagalog and Spanish).[4]

Rural Areas

Seventy per cent spoke only Tagalog at home, three per cent Tagalog and English, 8 per cent Ilocano, and 17 per cent Kapampango (due to the inclusion of a predominantly Pampango community, Santo Tomas).

Taking the combined urban and rural samples, about 58 per cent of all our respondents spoke only Tagalog with members of their household, and an additional 15 per cent spoke Tagalog and English at home; it is interesting to note that out of 640 respondents classified by language, 12 per cent spoke only English at home, and but 7 only Spanish. The failure of Spanish to achieve widespread usage in contrast to English is shown by the urban sample datum that for every five persons who speak Tagalog and Spanish at home, there are 95 who speak Tagalog and English!

Income

San Juan

Respondents were asked for the total monthly income of their household, so the following percentage figures are not for individual earnings (here and throughout, P=pesos):

	≤ P150	P151-300	P301-600	P601+	N*
males	29%	30%	25%	16%	441
females	23	27	35	15	77

*One per cent of the males and almost three per cent of the females gave no figures for their household income.

In other words, nearly 58 per cent of the males and females in our urban sample were in households with a total monthly income under P300.^{5} However, although official figures relating to data are lacking, it is probably safe to say that the average income of our sample is higher than for the rest of Filipino urban centers--but it is difficult to assert how much higher.

Respondents were also asked "How much do you think an average family--a man, his wife, and three children--needs a month in order to live just comfortably?" The following summarizes the answers:

≤ P150	P151-300	P301-600	P601+	N
21%	49%	25%	5%	519

Rural Areas

Below is presented in percentage terms the actual monthly income of rural respondents in our sample together with what they conceive to be the needed income for an average household of five members:

	< P150	P151-300	P301-600	P601+	N*
actual	83%	15%	2	-	119
needed	54	45	1	-	111

Persons who did not know the monthly income of their households or did not give a figure for the needed income are not included in these figures; these individuals amounted to 3 and 2 per cent, respectively, of the sample.

It may be noted that slightly over one third of all our rural respondents had monthly household earnings under P75 (about $25), but only 8 per cent of the respondents thought this was the needed income for an average household. About 82 per cent of the respondents placed their estimates of the needed income at P200 or less. It is obvious that there are large discrepancies in the average income of urban and rural respondents (and in their estimates of needed income), but it must be kept in mind that rural respondents have a much lower standard of living and do not need to make as many cash purchases as urban workers.

Employment Status

San Juan

Eighty-two per cent of the sample reported full-time employment, 10 per cent reported part-time employment, and only 8 per cent were unemployed at the time of the survey. By sex, the employment status is as follows:

	full-time	part-time	unemployed	total
males	372 (83%)	34 (8%)	42 (9%)	448
females	60 (76%)	17 (21.5%)	2 (2.5%)	79

Rural Areas

Nearly three out of four rural respondents reported full-employment status, an additional 10 per cent showed part-time status and 25 per cent were reported as unemployed. Of the 85 individuals who were full-time employed (out of a total of 114 rural respondents), 81 (or 95 per cent) were males. Thus, it seems that full employment is more problematical in the rural areas than in the urban sample, which bears out the agrarian situation of a surplus population with inadequate employment facilities.[6]

Occupational Distribution

San Juan

The total sample showed the following composition: 22 per cent were professionals and semi-professionals, 7 per cent were in the managerial and executive group, one per cent were farm owners and farm managers, 9 per cent small business and self-employed, 17 per cent clerical and sales, 12 per cent skilled workers and foremen, 17 per cent semi-skilled workers and operatives, 5 per cent unskilled workers and laborers, one per cent domestic servants, and 8 per cent public service workers. By sex the percentage distribution is as follows:

	Males (N=448)	Females (N=79)	All (N=527)
Professionals & semi-professionals	19%	37%	22%
Managers and executives	8.5	1	7
Farm owners and farm managers	2	-	1
Small business, self-employed	8	18	10
Clerical and sales workers	16.5	21.5	18
Skilled workers and foremen	14	1	12
Semi-skilled, operatives	17	18	17
Unskilled, laborers	5	2.5	4
Domestic servants	<.5	1	1
Public service workers	9	-	8
Not classifiable	<.5	-	-

Undoubtedly, the figures for professionals and semi-professionals, and also for managers and executives are a biased estimate of the total population; however, it must be kept in mind that San Juan is somewhat atypical of urban centers since it is an upper-middle class residential area, with many professionals such as physicians, lawyers, and teachers, working in nearby Manila. Quite likely, also, is that domestic servants may be underrepresented because interviews were mainly conducted with household heads; a domestic servant living with his employer (as is often the case) would not have an equal chance of being included in our survey.

Rural Areas

The occupational distribution for all the respondents and for full-time workers only is given below, in percentage terms:

	All workers (n=114)	Full-time workers (n=85)
Professionals and semi-professionals	3.5%	5%
Managers and executives	-	-
Farm owners and farm managers	14	13
Small business, self-employed	3	2
Clerical and sales workers	3	2
Skilled workers and foremen	10.5	12
Semi-skilled and kindred workers	17	19
Unskilled workers (incl. farm laborers)	14	12
Farm tenants	33	34
Not classifiable	3	1

For purposes of comparison, below are the percentage figures for household heads given by Rivera and McMillan in their survey:[7]

Professionals and semi-professionals	1.3%
Proprietors, managers, and officials	2.2
Sales persons and clerks	2.2
Skilled laborers	1.5
Semiskilled laborers	19.2
Unskilled laborers	10.2
Farm owners	25.7
Farm tenants	21.5
Farm laborers	9.5
No occupation	6.7

Nature of the Work Situation

A last measure of differentiation of individuals is a classification devised by the writer. The advantage of classifying respondents on the basis of their work situation--with their primary object of interaction--is that this cross-cuts occupational groups and attempts to find a meaningful common denominator, which is absent in accepted standard classifications. For analytical purposes, at least, four primary work situations were drawn: respondents were classified as being essentially in contact with people (e.g., teachers, sales workers, policemen, physicians), with machines and technological objects (factory workers, drivers, etc.), with non-technological material objects (farmers, miners, fishermen, etc.), and lastly, with abstractions and symbols (engineers, accountants, etc.). Concretely, there will be ambiguity in classifying certain individual s (for example, is a lawyer primarily in contact with people or primarily in contact with abstract principles of law?), and much emphasis was placed on what respondents described their total work situation to be. Those who could not be placed in one of these four groups were listed as non-classifiable. Below is shown the percentage figures for the urban and the rural samples.

	Urban	Rural
primarily in contact with people	37%	7%
primarily in contact with technological objects	31	25
primarily in contact with non-technological objects, with the physical environment	9	62
primarily in contact with symbols	18	3
not classifiable	5	3

This classification system is to be considered as still tentative; the criteria have not been completely standardized. But it seemed plausible to postulate that an individual's perception of the occupational structure is to some extent influenced by his primary source of interaction in his total work situation. Workers whose occupational roles place them primarily in contact with people may share more of a common outlook than those who are primarily in contact with technological objects, regardless of the particular occupation status.

Intergenerational Differences

For the urban respondents (N=442), a comparison was made between the longest held occupation of fathers and sons. The percentage results are the following:

Occupational Category	Fathers	Sons
Professionals and semi-professionals	13%	19%
Managerial and executive	6	9
Farm owners and tenants	26	2
Small business, self-employed	11	8
Clerical and sales	7	17
Skilled workers and foremen	12	14
Semiskilled workers	9	17
Unskilled workers	4	5
Public service workers	12	9

With two exceptions, some had fathers engaged in farming more than in any other occupational group. The two exceptions were professionals and semi-professionals, who tended to come from professional homes more than any other category, and unskilled workers, who had fathers engaged in semi-skilled work more than any other form of employment. Of public service workers twenty-nine per cent had fathers in the same category and 27 per cent had fathers occupied in farming. However, it appears that more sons had fathers engaged in the same occupational group as they than any other group. With this proviso, there is a greater likelihood of a son being in his father's occupational group (but not a specific occupation) than his going into any other single group. But in no occupational group was the likelihood of sons' going into their fathers' occupational status greater (i.e., over 50 per cent) than their going into all other groups; the highest percentage of inherited occupational status was for professionals and semi-professionals, 37 per cent of whom had fathers in a similar position. The great amount of sons having fathers in farming gives an indication of rural to urban migration; out of 442 respondents, 114 (26 per cent) had fathers whose longest-held occupation was farming. The most pronounced intergenerational differences are the decline of workers engaged in farming, and the increase of clerical and sales workers, as well as semi-skilled workers.

Another inter-generational comparison is between the place of birth of children and their fathers. For San Juan respondents the following percentages were found.

	place of birth				
	barrio	town	city	other*	don't know
fathers	8%	71%	14%	3%	4%
children	4	71	24	1	-

(*"other" refers to outside the Philippines)

The actual frequencies are presented below:

		respondents' birthplace				
		barrio	town	city	other	N
fathers'	barrio	18	17	5	-	40
birthplace	town	1	48	324	1	374
	city	-	8	64	1	73
	other	-	7	5	4	16
	don't know	-	18	6	-	24
	total	19	374	128	6	527

From these figures, it appears that respondents were more likely to be born in the same type of locality as their father than any other type; this is especially marked in respondents born in cities (88 per cent of whose fathers were born in cities) and those born in towns (87 per cent had fathers born in towns).

SUBJECTIVE CHARACTERISTICS

Comparison to Father

Respondents were asked, "Do you think, you have had more, the same, or less education than your father?" The urban and rural samples were broken down into two groups, those under 40 years of age and those 40 and above.

	Urban Sample				
	more	same	less	don't know	N
under 40	191	39	52	11	293
	(65%)	(13%)	(18%)	(4%)	
40 and over	167	31	23	12	233
	(72%)	(13%)	(10%)	(5%)	

	Rural Sample				
under 40	41	11	8	-	60
	(68%)	(18%)	(13%)		
40 and over	34	16	4	-	54
	(63%)	(30%)	(7%)		

The main finding is the large majority of respondents in both urban and rural samples who think they have gotten a better education than their fathers.   Undoubtedly, the spread and development of mass public education, largely the result of the American administration (1899-1946), is reflected in our figures. In San Juan 72 per cent (18 out of 25) of those 60 years old and over reported having had more education than their fathers; this age group was the first to feel the development of mass education, which made the contrast with their preceding generation even greater. Unfortunately we do not have enough cases in our sample of those who were brought up during the Spanish regime, but it is likely that intergenerational differences in educational achievement were smaller than during the post-Spanish period.

Another question posed was "On the whole, do you consider yourself better off, the same as, or worse off socially and economically than your father when he was the same age as you are now?" Results for the total sample, by age groups, are as follows:

	better	same	worse	don't know	N
under 40	149	86	91	28	354
	(42%)	(24%)	(26%)	(8%)	
40 and above	150	63	56	17	286
	(52%)	(22%)	(20%)	(6%)	

It appears that not only do more respondents feel that they are better off than were their fathers at the same age but also that older respondents see themselves as being in a better position in relation to their fathers than younger respondents do.

The urban respondents were classified into white-collar and blue-collar workers with the following comparison to their fathers:

	better	same	worse	d.k.	N
white-collar	165	59	56	22	302
	(55%)	(19.5%)	(18.5%)	(7%)	
blue-collar	93	60	68	19	240
	(39%)	(25%)	(28%)	(8%)	

($x2$ with 3 d.f. is significant at or beyond the .01 level)

From this it appears that white-collar workers see themselves better off than their fathers to a degree which is significantly higher than blue-collar workers.

Type of Work Preferred

All respondents were asked, "If you had to choose between doing manual labor or mental work, which would you choose?"

manual	mental	both	d.k.	n.a.*	N
216	389	18	11	6	640
(34%)	(61%)	(3%)	(2%)	(1%)	

(*n.a. denotes no answer or not applicable)

The total sample was divided into white-collar and blue-collar workers with the following results:

	manual	mental	both	d.k.	n.a.	N
white-collar	66	240	13	3	5	327
	(20%)	(73%)	(4%)	(1%)	(2%)	
blue-collar	148	147	4	8	1	308
	(48%)	(48%)	(1%)	(3%)	(<.5%)	

While blue-collar workers seem nearly equally divided between choosing manual labor or mental work, white-collar workers prefer mental work to manual labor by a better than 3:1 ratio. This difference between respondents is statistically significant.

Work Satisfaction

All the individuals in our sample were asked, "On the whole, would you say that you feel very satisfied, satisfied, indifferent, dissatisfied, or very dissatisfied with your present occupation?" The results were:

	% of responses	Number of persons
very satisfied	19	121
satisfied	61	389
indifferent	1	5
dissatisfied	12	75
very dissatisfied	2	10
don't know	1	6
no answer/not applicable	4	25
total	100	631

The total sample was broken down by age (under 40, 40 and over) and into blue-collar and white-collar workers. No significant differences were found by age within either of the latter two, but between them the results are the following:

	white-collar	blue-collar
very satisfied	28%	10%
satisfied	60	63
indifferent	1	-
dissatisfied	6	18
very dissatisfied	1	2
don't know	1	1
no answer/not classifiable	3	6

Although a substantial majority of both white-collar and blue-collar workers feel either satisfied or very satisfied with their jobs, it appears that three times as many white-collar workers are very satisfied as blue-collar workers, and that three times as many blue-collar workers are dissatisfied or very dissatisfied as white-collar workers.

Wide differences as far as level of job satisfaction were found by specific occupational groups (see Appendix, Table 2). Managers and executives had the highest percentage of those very satisfied (46 per cent) and unskilled workers the lowest (only 1 out of 42); among those who said they were dissatisfied with their job, farm tenants (28 per cent) and unskilled workers (26 per cent) were highest, with managers and executives (5 per cent) and farm owners and managers (5 per cent) the lowest.

Respondents were also asked what they liked best about their present occupations; their spontaneous responses were grouped with the following results:

	Per cent of total
intrinsic work satisfaction	17
working conditions (environment, hours, independence, etc.)	12
wages, economic security	11
work associates	6
nearness to home	6
prestige of the job or occupation	3
opportunities for advancement or educational opportunities of the job	3
employer and supervisors	1
other reasons	5
don't know	4
no spontaneous responses	32
total	100

A comparison between white-collar and blue-collar workers is shown below (in percentage figures):

	white-collar	blue-collar
intrinsic work satisfaction	16%	17%
working conditions	15	9
wages, economic security	10	12
work associates	7	6
nearness to home	5	6
prestige of the job or occupation	4	<1
opportunities for advancement	4	3
employer and supervisors	<1	2
other reasons	7	3
don't know	4	5
no spontaneous responses	28	37
total	100%	100%

On the whole, there appears to be no major differences between factors cited by white-collar and blue-collar workers. It may be noted that less than one percent of the total sample mentioned service to the country or the community as the factor liked best in the occupation.

Work Dissatisfaction

What do workers dislike most about their jobs? The percentage figures for white-collar workers, blue-collar workers, and the total sample are presented below:

	All responses*	white-collar	blue-collar
wages, economic insecurity	9%	7%	10%
working conditions	8	9	7
distances from home	5	6	4
employer and supervisors	4	2	7
work associates	3	2	3
lack of opportunities for advancement or education	3	1	5
lack of intrinsic work satisfaction (boredom, monotony)	2	2	2
low prestige of the job	1	1	1
other reasons	10	13	8
don't know	6	8	5
no spontaneous responses	49	49	48
total	100%	100%	100%

(*includes persons unemployed who were asked about their previous longest-held occupation)

Since the majority of all respondents had indicated satisfaction with their occupation, it is not too surprising to find a large percentage of non-responses. On the whole, there are no major differences between white-collar and blue-collar workers, but blue-collar workers mention *employer and supervisors* and also *lack of opportunities* more often than white-collar workers.

Occupation Preferred

All the respondents were given the following question, "If you had the chance to do so, in what occupation would you like to be (what kind of work would you like to do?)." The sample was broken down into white-collar and blue-collar workers with the following percentages:

occupation preferred	white-collar respondents (N = 327)	blue-collar respondents (N=308)
same occupation as now	25%	16%
professional, semi-professional	26	8
managerial and executive	10	3
farming (farm owner, etc.)	4	6
small business, self-employed	14	10
clerical and sales	7	12
skilled worker and foreman	2	15
semi-skilled worker and kindred	1	8
unskilled worker	1	2
public service worker	-	1
don't know	5	12
no answer or not classifiable	5	7
total	100%	100%

If among San Juan respondents we omit those who answered "don't know" or whose answers were not classifiable, and group occupations preferred in terms of white-collar occupations (professional and semi-professionals, managerial and executive, small-business and self-employed, clerical and sales) and blue-collar occupations (skilled, semi-skilled, unskilled, and public service), then the following comparison can be made between white-collar and blue-collar workers:[8]

Respondents	Occupation Preferred			
	same	white-collar	blue-collar	N
white-collar	82	187	12	281
	(29%)	(67%)	(4%)	
blue-collar	50	101	80	231
	(22%)	(44%)	(34%)	
all	132	288	92	512
	(26%)	(56%)	(18%)	

The survey also asked, "What occupation would you advise your children to enter, assuming they had the chance to do so?" The results, for white-collar and blue-collar respondents are given in the following table:

Occupation preferred	white-collar respondents	blue-collar respondents	both
professional, semi-professional	41%	30%	36%
managerial and executive	1	<1	1
farming	4	6	4
small business, self-employed	11	7	9
clerical and sales	2	8	5
skilled worker and foreman	2	10	6
semi-skilled	1	6	3
public service	<1	<1	<1
their own choice	29	20	24
don't know	4	8	6
not applicable, not classifiable	5	5	5

The high parental aspiration for the professions ("my son the doctor" or "my son the lawyer") contrasts with a very low degree of parental aspiration for the modern industrial sector (managerial and executive). This is a neglected avenue of social mobility.

Whereas wages or economic security was mentioned by only 11 per cent of the total sample as far as what is liked best about the *actual* occupation, 26 per cent of the total sample mentioned this factor as the main reason for the *desired* occupation. This difference is even more marked if we consider the reasons given by respondents for the occupation they would like their children to enter:

Reasons for desired children's occupation	white-collar respondents (N=237)*	blue-collar respondents (N=308)*
wages, economic security	27%	40%
service to the country/community	18	13
prestige of the occupation	7	5
opportunities for advancement	7	4
working conditions	4	7
intrinsic work satisfaction	1	<.5
nearness to home	0	2
work associates	0	<.5
other reasons	34	29
don't know	2	0

*Respondents who left the choices of occupation up to their children are not included; this amounted to about 25 per cent of the total sample.

In addition to the emphasis placed on *economic security*, service to the country (or to the community) was the second most frequently mentioned reason, by both blue-collar and white-collar workers. For their actual occupation, respondents had mentioned *intrinsic work satisfaction* and *working conditions* most frequently in respect to what they liked best, but these, as we have seen, are not the main factors in deciding what occupation they would like their children to have.

A final comparison was made between the reason given for one's desired occupation and for one's children. Of the 168 persons in the combined sample (blue-collar and white-collar) who had mentioned *wages* or *economic security* as the reason for their own desired occupation, 65 (39 per cent) mentioned this as the reason for the occupation they would advise their children to enter; this was by far the most frequently mentioned factor, with the second, *service to the country*, mentioned by only 11 per cent. Those who liked best about their desired occupation the *working conditions* nevertheless mentioned *wages* as the reason for their children's occupation more than any other factor (22 per cent, with *working conditions* mentioned by 9 per cent of the respondents). Those who had indicated *intrinsic work satisfaction or opportunities for advancement* for their own desired occupation still mentioned *wages* as the most frequently mentioned reason for their children's occupation. Of course, in evaluating the importance of *wages* or *economic security* one is not certain whether this is a projective mechanism at work (i.e., whether the respondent does not admit wages as his own personal source of work satisfaction but projects this desire or motivation to his son's occupation) or whether the respondents are thinking in terms of the best interest of their children, or whether there is a combination of both. It would also seem that those respondents who find their prime work satisfaction in non-material aspects (e.g., *prestige of the occupation*, service to the country) are consistent in stressing non-material factors for choosing their children's occupation.

In summarizing this section on the subjective aspects of the occupational structure, we can point to the following main conclusions:

(1) a majority of individuals prefer white-collar occupations to blue-collar occupations, and particularly the professions to any other single occupational group,

(2) on the whole both white-collar and blue-collar workers see themselves as better off than their fathers, and

(3) a great majority of both white-collar and blue-collar workers feel satisfied or very satisfied with their present occupation.[9]

With this background, we can turn to the prestige evaluation of occupational roles, which will be treated in the following chapter.

NOTES

1. Because of the population increase since 1948, our percentages are probably somewhat smaller.

2. Before World War II *elementary* schooling comprised four years of *primary* and three years of *intermediate* education. Since the war elementary schooling has been reduced by one year. Secondary or high school education was before the war, and still is, a four-year program.

3. Figures cited in Rivera and McMillan, *The Rural Philippines*, p. 166.

4. Language spoken at home does not exclude the respondent's familiarity with other tongues.

5. Officially the peso is equivalent to fifty U.S. cents, but the unofficial (free) rate is one peso=$.33.

6. In their study of nine barrios in Central Luzon, Rivera and McMillan found 32 per cent of the male labor force unemployed (*An Economic and Social Survey of Rural Households in Central Luzon*, p. 113).

7. *The Rural Philippines*, p. 211.

8. Farming as an occupational choice is not included in these figures because of its ambiguity: a person may wish to be in farming as a farm owner or manager who employs tenants and as such be considered a white-collar individual; another respondent may mean by farming a desire to till the soil himself and hence could be considered as blue-collar. Five per cent of San Juan males indicated farming as an occupational choice.

9. One possible reason for the latter finding is the fact that unemployment and underemployment are grim realities in Central Luzon so that someone who has a job will feel more satisfied with it in comparing himself with unemployed workers than if he were living in an economy of full employment.

CHAPTER V

THE EVALUATION OF OCCUPATIONS

RANKING OF OCCUPATIONS

Respondents were first grouped according to the number of occupations ranked. The frequency distribution is given below:

		0	1-5	6-10	11-15	16-20	21-25	26-29	30	N
Number of occupations ranked										
urban		6	4	4	5	1	8	13	482	523
rural		-	4	10	6	1	1	5	84	111
all		6	8	14	11	2	9	18	566	634

Given the initial inexperience of our interviewers and the unfamiliarity of respondents with public opinion surveys (as discussed in Chapter III), it was gratifying that 89 per cent of the total sample were able to rank all 30 occupations, and 92 per cent were able to evaluate at least 26 occupations; on the other hand, only 2 per cent of all the respondents could not rank more than five occupations. In the urban sample, 92 per cent were able to rank all 30 occupations against 76 per cent of the combined rural sample.

In the urban sample, those respondents who were not able to rank all 30 occupations appeared to be randomly distributed as far as socio-economic status. As far as educational achievement, only about one-fifth had not gone beyond a primary education, and two-fifths of those who had failed to rank 30 occupations had gone beyond a high school education. In terms of occupational status and monthly household income, the distribution of those who had not rated all the occupations was also widespread. In the rural sample, as well, there was no marked discrepancy between the socio-economic status of those unable to evaluate all 30 occupations and those who could do so.

In view of the fact that an overwhelming majority of respondents were able to rank all 30 occupations, it was thought feasible to concentrate on this group for computational purposes in data analysis; hence, unless otherwise noted, we have based our calculations on this category. Of course, if it were the case that those who did not rank all 30 occupations perceived the occupational structure differently from those who did, then we would be introducing a bias into our results. However, the rank correlation coefficient between those who ranked 11-29 occupations and those who ranked all 30 was, for all occupations, +.98, showing a very high degree of agreement.[1]

We first present the rank evaluation for all the respondents (N = 606) who ranked 11-30 occupations:

Occupation	Final rank
physician	1
congressman	2
lawyer	3
engineer	4
university professor	5
priest	6
manager of a business company	7
officer in the armed forces	8
intermediate school teacher	9
professional artist	10
farmer	11
midwife	12
office clerk	3
policeman	14
enlisted man	15.5

owner of a sari-sari store	15.5
salesman	17
tailor	18
fisherman	19
carpenter	20
farm tenant	21
construction worker	22
factory worker	23
sugar plantation worker	24
barber	25.5
bus driver	25.5
gas station attendant	27
road repairman	28
produce peddler	29
domestic servant	30

(*the total sum of ranks for a given occupation was divided by the number of respondents who had rated it in order to obtain the mean rank value; the final rank represents the position of the mean rank of a given occupation vis-à-vis all other mean ranks.)

Although the interpretation of this ranking will occur later, it may be pointed out at this point that the top third consists mainly of professional status occupations and that the bottom third is comprised chiefly of semi\skilled and unskilled occupations. It may also be pointed us that this ranking is practically identical with the one of those who rated *all* the items.[2]

Age

The ranking of respondents under 40 years of age was compared with that of respondents over 40. The rank correlation coefficient[3] of the occupational rankings between the two groups was .99. The greatest rank difference for a given occupation was found for *farmer* and for *office clerk*; those under 40 years of age rated *office clerk* three ranks higher than did those over 40, and the latter rated *farmer* three ranks higher than the former.

Sex

The rank correlation coefficient of the occupational rankings of men and women was .98; women rated *university professor* three ranks higher than men, and men rated *construction worker* four ranks lower than women. The only other difference involving as much as three ranks was for *congressman*, who was ranked second by men and fifth by women.

Locality

Relative to other indices, locality was an index which differentiated respondents as far as their agreement on the ranking of occupations, but the correlation coefficient of .96 between the urban and the combined rural sample is still very high. The correlation between Nangka respondents and San Juan respondents in regard to the occupational ranking was .96, between all the other rural areas and San Juan .95, and between Nangka and all other rural areas .97. (Santo Tomas, the Pampango-speaking community, showed a similar high level of agreement with Tagalog-speaking areas.) Urban respondents rated *fisherman* seven ranks higher than rural respondents and the latter rated *factory worker* five ranks higher than the former; these were the largest rank differences.

Religion

Respondents were grouped in terms of four categories: a) Roman Catholic, b) Aglipayan and Iglesia ni Kristo, c) Protestant, and d) other religions or none. The various correlation coefficients are given below:

	Roman Catholic	Aglipayan & I.ni Kristo	Protestant	none & other
Catholic	--	.98	.975	.96
Aglipayan & I.ni Kristo		--	.955	.95
Protestant			--	.94
None & other				--

The average correlation for the six pairs involved was .96.

Those grouped under *none and all other* tended to place *farmer* seven to nine ranks lower than other groups did, but they also placed *farm tenant* five to eight ranks higher than other respondents. Protestants ranked *priest* fifth, and Catholics ranked that occupation sixth; its lowest rating came from members of Aglipayan and Iglesia ni Kristo who gave it a rating of ninth.

Income

Respondents were also divided into four categories in terms of their monthly household income: P150 or less, P151-300, P301-600, P601>.

The intercorrelations are the following:

	P150 or less	P151-300	P301-600	P601>
P150 or less	--	.99	.99	.98
P151-300		--	.99	.98
P301-600			--	.98
P601>				--

Only two occupations had as many as four rank differences between groups: *carpenter* was rated twenty-third by those having the wealthiest households and nineteenth by the poorest earners and also by those in the P301-600 category; *manager of a business company* received its highest rating (third) from those earning P601> and lowest (seventh) from those in the P151-300 category.

Education

Education *per se* does not seem to differentiate people's perspectives of the occupational prestige hierarchy. Respondents were divided into those who had not gone beyond primary school, those who had gone beyond primary but not beyond high school, and those who had gone beyond high school.

The rank correlation coefficient for each of the three possible pairs was .99, with a rank difference of three being the highest observed between groups.

Occupational Status

First, a broad division was made between blue-collar and white-collar workers, which yielded a correlation coefficient of .99--so there is very high agreement between the two as to the ranking of occupations; this is shown by the fact that only one occupation, *farmer*, involved the two groups in a rank difference of three (farmer was rated 11th by white-collar workers and 14th by blue-collar workers).

Correlation coefficients were also obtained for pairs of specific occupational groups:[4]

	I	II	III	IV	V	VI	VII	VIII	IX	X
I	--	.97	.96	.98	.99	.99	.98	.96	.99	.94
II		--	.95	.97	.96	.96	.96	.92	.96	.92
III			--	.97	.95	.96	.97	.94	.97	.97
IV				--	.98	.98	.98	.96	.98	.92
V					--	.99	.99	.96	.98	.92
VI						--	.99	.97	.98	.94
VII							--	.97	.99	.94
VIII								--	.97	.93
IX									--	.94
X										--

It can be noticed that farm tenants (group X) had the lowest correlations with other groups, its average correlation being .94; the highest correlation for farm tenants was .97 with farmers and farm owners (group III). The average rank correlation coefficient for all 45 pairs was .96.

Languages

Respondents were placed into four categories of language spoken at home; 1) Tagalog, 2) Tagalog and Spanish; Tagalog and English, 3) native languages other than Tagalog, and 4) Spanish or English.[5]   The rank correlation coefficients for occupational rankings between these four groups are as follows:

	1	2	3	4
1	--	.99	.95	.94
2		--	.93	.94
3			--	.92
4				--

The average correlation coefficient was .95. The lowest correlation was between persons who spoke native languages other than Tagalog and those who spoke Spanish or English--in other words, these two groups may be said to share the least cultural similarities, so it is possible that they perceive the occupational structure differently. However, it must be kept in mind that this comparison is only relative to the other groups, because a correlation of .92 is nevertheless very high.

Nature of the work situation

Using the four categories we have described elsewhere (primarily in contact with people, with technological objects, with non-technological objects, or with symbols and abstractions), we computed rank correlation coefficients for every pair and found the average rho to be .98. The highest correlation being between persons primarily in contact with symbols (rho = .99), and the lowest correlation being between those primarily in contact with non-technological objects and those primarily in contact with symbols (.978). For any pair, the rank difference of any given occupation was not greater than three. Contrary to our expectation, this criterion does not seem to differentiate workers' perception of the occupational structure.

Although we could have used other variables, it is quite clear that regardless of the index selected, there is a very high consensus of agreement as to the overall ranking. This conclusion is very much in keeping with other studies outside of the Philippines.

It is interesting to note that regardless of the criterion we used to differentiate the sample, *physician* always rates at the top (first) and *domestic servant* always ranks last (thirtieth). Theoretically, this may be due to two reasons: first, most people place *physician* first and *domestic servant* last, and/or second, the range of variation of the prestige rank of these occupations is relatively small. To the writer's knowledge, this problem has not been systematically investigated in previous studies. To test this out we considered the frequencies for occupations ranked first and last, with the following results:

Occupations most often ranked first and last

A. Ranked first		B. Ranked last	
occupation	frequency	occupation	frequency
congressman	177	road repairman	93
physician	103	produce peddler	76
priest	80	barber	55
lawyer	61	gas sta. attendant	55
business mgr.	58	bus driver	53
professor	52	sugar plant. worker	41
engineer	52	domestic servant	32
farmer	41	factory worker	26
officer	30	construction worker	25

If we compare these frequencies with the rank evaluation for all respondents who graded 11 occupations or more, we notice the following:

a) on the whole, occupations most frequently mentioned first and last, respectively, are the same as those whose average rank is near the top or the bottom, but

b) there is no one-to-one correspondence between the number of times an occupation was placed first (or last) and its average rank. Thus, although *congressman* was ranked first by many more people, its *average rank* placed it below *physician*; likewise, although *domestic servant* was placed last by fewer persons than six other occupations, its average rank is definitely lower than all other occupations. There are also some interesting rural-urban differences as to the relative frequencies of occupations ranked first:

Rural		Urban	
occupation	frequency	occupation	frequency
congressman	29	congressman	148
priest	12	physician	92
physician	11	priest	68
farmer	11	business manager	58
officer	8	lawyer	54
lawyer	7	professor	50

On the basis of these frequencies, *farmer* and *officer* are more "prestigeful" in rural areas than in the urban sample; on the other hand, *manager of a business company*, which had the fourth highest number of first place mentions in the urban sample, failed to be ranked first by any rural person.[6]

We then calculated the standard deviation of each occupation from its mean rank value (see Appendix, Table 5) having divided the sample of respondents ranking all 30 occupations into two groups: those under 40 years of age and those over 40 years old. The rank correlation coefficient between the two sets of standard deviations is .77. This shows that there is essential agreement between the two age groups as to the variation in the ranks assigned to particular occupations. The occupations which showed the greatest discrepancy in the ranks of their standard deviation for the two groups were, in that order, *salesman, midwife, policeman, road repairman,* and *domestic servant.* Persons under 40 were more uniform in ranking *salesman, policeman,* and *domestic servant* than those 40 years of age or over.

Physician had the lowest standard deviation in both groups, 3.88 and 4.02 respectively. On the other hand, *farmer* had the highest standard deviation in both groups, 7.45 and 7.13. *Enlisted man in the armed forces, farm tenant,* and *congressman* had large standard deviations for both age groups, whereas *engineer, barber,* and *tailor* had relatively low standard deviations in both cases. It seems that on the whole, agrarian occupations *(farmer, fisherman, farm tenant)* show the greatest spread in their rankings; this might well be a common feature in societies in the process of transition from an agrarian base economy into an industrial system. The low purchasing power of these occupations, on the one hand, and their traditional status as the "backbone" of the country, on the other hand, help to make them foci of ambiguity as to their prestige standing: the greater the ambiguity, the greater the spread of the ranking for any given occupation.

What appears to be of significant interest is that the average standard deviation from the mean rank of an occupation is rather high for both age groups. Previous studies have tended to emphasize the very high agreement as to the overall rank or overall score of given occupational roles; but our data suggest that there is *noticeable variation between individual respondents as to the relative position of any given occupation.* To account for this, it seems plausible to suggest that, in the Philippines at least, respondents have a plurality of prestige reference systems indicative of a plurality of value-orientations. If everyone shared the same prestige frame of reference, then we should expect for each occupation a relatively small standard deviation (as a measure of dispersion) from its mean rank, but this does not appear to be the case. If our inference is correct, what are the frames of reference used by individuals in ranking occupations?

SUBJECTIVE FRAMES OF REFERENCE

For each of the top three and bottom three rated occupations, respondents were asked the reason(s) why they had placed a particular occupation in that position. The various reasons were grouped into several categories; in case of more than one reason for a given occupation, we tried to select the one most emphasized or stressed by the respondent. Below is given the percentage distribution of reasons for occupations ranked first:

Descriptive category	Percentage
1. functional importance or service to country, community or mankind in general	25
2. income, economic security, standard of living	18
3. social prestige in the community	14
4. education and other requirements needed	11
5. power or influence of the occupation	5
6. nobility of the work	4
7. functional importance or service to others, individuals or groups of individuals	4
8. reference group (respondent is, has been, or expects to be in the occupation, or knows someone in it)	3
9. opportunities for advancement, springboard to other occupations	2
10. independence from others	1
11. moral character of persons in the occupation	1
12. other reasons	10
13. don't know, no reason given	2

In the rural sample *congressman* (placed first twice more often than the next occupation) had *power* or *influence* mentioned more than any other reason for its high prestige (*income* was mentioned next); in the urban sample, *functional importance to the country* was mentioned more frequently than anything else as the reason for placing *congressman* first (*general prestige in the community* was second in frequency). *Functional importance to the country* (or the community, or people in general) was also given most frequently for the following occupations placed first by urban as well as rural respondents *farmer, officer in the armed forces, physician,* and *priest.* For *university professor* and *lawyer* the reason cited most often was *education and other requirements needed.* Income had the highest frequency of responses for *manager of a business company* and *engineer.* It would be interesting to see whether in formerly colonial countries an awakening nationalism and aroused patriotic feelings is the main factor which tends to make *functional importance to the nation or the community* the most important frame of reference for judging an occupation's prestige standing.

What are the frames of reference used by respondents in ranking an occupation last? It was found possible to group the various responses into categories which are really the converse of those used in rating an occupation at the top, e.g., an occupation may be placed last because of its low functional significance to the country, because of its low income, its few opportunities or lack of opportunities for advancement, etc. We have suggested that each category constitutes a frame of reference used in evaluating an occupation; each category can be conceived as embodying a certain continuum so that the respondent can score an occupation high or low along this continuum, depending upon whether he is placing an occupation at the top or at the bottom of the prestige hierarchy. This conception suggests that there are essentially the same frames of reference used in placing an occupation at the top as there are in evaluating an occupation at the bottom. But, *in evaluating top occupations a different frame of reference may be emphasized from that used in rating bottom occupations.* This is given below in the percentage distribution of reasons given in placing an occupation last.

Descriptive category	Percentages
1. income, economic insecurity, standard of living	24
2. degradation or ignobility of the work	14
3. social prestige in the community	11
4. low or absence of education and other requirements	9
5. dependence on others, no freedom of expression	9
6. working conditions	7
7. low functional importance to the country, etc.	5
8. no opportunities for advancement, a "dead-end"	5

9. moral character of persons in the occupation   3
10. low functional importance to others, to individuals   1
11. personal dislike for persons in that occupation   1
12. other reasons   10
13. don't know, no reason given   1

The economic frame of reference (*income, standard of living, economic insecurity*) was most used by persons ranking last the following occupations: *produce peddler, gasoline station attendant, bus driver, barber, factory worker, fisherman,* and *plantation worker.* For *road repairman, construction worker,* and *enlisted man in the armed forces,* the factor of unfavorable *working conditions* was used more than any other.

Why a particular frame of reference is more emphasized in placing an occupation at the top than in placing an occupation at the bottom of the prestige hierarchy is an interesting question, but unfortunately this problem falls outside the scope of our study.

In connection with the subjective frames of reference, one finding of our survey is the fact that not only do different individuals tend to use different frames of reference, but also that the same individual may simultaneously entertain different ones. To illustrate this, we shall present some *verbatim* responses given by a cross-section of our respondents when they were asked the reasons for placing in the top three and bottom three positions the occupations they did.

<u>rank</u> <u>occupation</u>   <u>reasons</u>

from a carpenter:
1   farmer   "He supports the nation"
2   officer   "He is the defense of the nation"
3   farm tenant   "He helps the farmer in supporting the nation"
28   policeman   "Most policemen are corrupt and dishonest"
29   domestic servant   "He has no education and no chance for improvement"
30   congressman   "He is corrupt and not good for the people"

from a physician:
1   congressman   "He is the most important figure in our society--some sort of ideal"
2   lawyer/physician "His profession is considered one of the best in our country"

3	manager/business company	"He earns a lot of money, and we go for people who have lots of money"
28	farm tenant	"He is another remnant of Spanish colonization"
29	gas sta.attendant	"A useless, worthless product of the car age and modern invention"
30	domestic servant	"He is a marked remnant of Spanish colonization in the Philippines"

from a night watchman:

1	farmer	"The most important occupation. It [has] existed forever, and life in this world is dependent upon the farmer"
2	farm tenant	"It is a great help in improving the economic condition of this country"
3	fisherman	"It is a job which I think is very hard. You are not sure if you would earn too much money"
28	engineer	"It has more knowledge, and important for this occupation, requires money"
29	professor	"It is a job which also requires much money before you can be one of it. Rarely possessed by the common masses"
30	congressman	"It is a job which the 'common tao'[people] could not get"

from an engineer:

1	officer	"He is the saviour and source of defense of the country"
2	enlisted man	"He helps the officers of the armed forces. Without him, they can't operate well"
3	lawyer	"He helps in the settling . . . of disputes"
28	barber	"He is the servant of all, poor or young; besides his earning can't cope with the social level of other occupations"
29	produce peddler	"His ways of earning deviate him from all the occupations"
30	domestic servant	"He or she is a servant of all"

from a salesman:
1   farmer   "He supports the nation"
2   fisherman   "He supplies us with fish"
3   construc. worker   "He repairs and makes our shelter"
28   lawyer   "He is not important, and . . . cannot do
                        anything for the community"
29   gas sta.attendant "He is also not important; even though they
                        are absent, we can live"
30   bus/jeepney driver"He can be absent, but still the community
                        can get along"

from a municipal clergy:
1   congressman   "They enjoy high respect from the people"
2   physician   "They are supposed to be the guardian of
                        our health"
3   manager of   "They are big people in business"
     business company
28   produce peddler"They earn very little"
29   road repairman   "They are the poorest workers in the public
                        works"
30   domestic servant   "They don't earn enough"

from an insurance agent:
1   priest   "He is the only one who can bring us close
                        to God"
2   congressman   "He is a representative of the people in the
                        government"
3   farmer   "He gives us food"
28   bus/jeepney driver"He is economically unstable and [has] low
                        social status"
29   produce peddler"He does not have a chance to study"
30   domestic servant   "This job is for those who can't afford
                        anything, not even an education"

from a hospital ward attendant:
1   congressman   "He is the lawmaker"
2   physician   "He needs a long time for obtaining an
                        education"
3   priest   "He preaches goodness and right living"
28   barber   "a little or no education"
29   gas sta.attendant "very low income and low social status"
30   domestic servant   "He has no education"

from a radio technician:

1	farmer	"He produces our food"
2	owner of sari- sari store	"Invest a little and it will increase"
3	profes'nal artist	"It promotes joy and happiness to mankind"
28	domestic servant	"It is a job for the lazy"
29	salesman	"It is an easy job"
30	barber	"Even if you don't have a haircut it will do"

from a rentier:

1	physician	"renders many services to the community"
2	priest	"takes care of the spiritual life of the people"
3	policeman	"promotes peace and order in the community"
28	enlisted man	"does not need any training"
29	owner of sari- sari store	"has a very low income"
30	congressman	"does not render any benefits to the people . . . does nothing but talk and talk in Congress"

PERCEPTION OF OCCUPATIONAL GROUPINGS

A final aspect of the occupational structure which our study attempted to cover is whether respondents perceive definite occupational groups, and if so, how these groups are related to the prestige hierarchy.   To find this out we gave the following instructions (after the ranking of individual occupations):

Now please group together those occupations in which people are pretty much alike, are interested in the same things, lead abo ut the same kind of life, and are on the whole considered as soci al equals. You can place the occupations in as few or in as many groups as you like. if you cannot place an occupation in a group with others, put it aside as forming a group by itself.

We would like you to arrange these groups according to their average social standing, just like you did for each occupation . . . If you cannot place one group in such an order, leave it out.

The interviewers were also instructed to find out what the various occupations in a given group have in common, what is their "common denominator," and to indicate this information alongside each listed group.

Below is shown the percentage distribution of occupational groups perceived by respondents who rated all 30 occupations and for those who rated less than this.

	Respondents who ranked	
No. of groups perceived	all 30 (N=558)	less than 30 (N=72)
0	3%	18%
1	0	0
2	8	10
3	21	15
4	21	12
5	14	18
6	10	10
7	6	4
8	6	3
9 or more	11	10
total	100%	100%

It can be seen that 47 per cent of those having rated all occupations perceived five or more occupational groups, as against 45 per cent for those who had been unable to evaluate all 30 occupations. Of those who had rated all the occupations, 50 per cent of rural respondents perceived five or more occupational groups compared to 45 per cent of urban respondents. By occupational grouping, exclusive of persons in agriculture (farmers, farm managers, farm tenants), 46 per cent of both blue-collar and white-collar workers perceived five or more occupational groups. On the other hand, 61 per cent of those involved in agriculture listed five or more occupational groupings. The highest number of groups mentioned was 16, listed by only one individual.

To quantify the number and type of occupations listed in individual groups, and the common denominators mentioned for each group, would have been too laborious and time-consuming. But we can point out some qualitative aspects of this grouping. Among respondents who mentioned only two groups, the dichotomy tended to be on the basis of mental versus manual labor, with the former evaluated more highly.

With more than two groupings it is quite difficult to find definite patterns, although some are repeated more often than others. One pattern is to arrange occupations into groups by their socio-economic status (with the economic factor usually stressed), another, by the amount of training needed, or by the functional importance of occupations in the group for essential needs. These and others may be simultaneously used by one respondent.

Perhaps the most general conclusion we can make is that, just as in the case of evaluating individual occupations, there is no unidimensional stratification of occupational groups according to their prestige. On the whole not only do different respondents have very varied systems of occupational grouping, but the same respondent, more often than not, will not group occupations according to a single variable (such as income, education, working conditions). Yet, it must be stressed that even if a respondent has various frames of reference in grouping occupations, he is able to hierarchize these different groups.

What also seems to be the case, according to our findings, is that there is a positive association between an occupation being ranked at or near the top and its being placed in a group which is ranked high, but this does not necessarily mean that a respondent who has rated an occupation at the top will place it in the occupational group deemed to have the highest social standing. Also, the reason why a particular occupation is rated at the top is not the same as the common denominator given for the group in which it is placed, whether that group is ranked first or not. For example, one respondent ranked *manager of a business company* second out of 30 because of its *high salary*; he placed it in an occupational group with *congressman* and *officer in the armed forces* because these three have responsibility. Another individual who had ranked *physician* third because "he serves humanity," placed this occupation in a group whose common denominator was "social and economic prestige."

In the next and closing chapter, we shall attempt to summarize our findings concerning the occupation structure of the Philippines and the prestige evaluation of occupational roles. We shall also compare our data with that of previously reported studies.

NOTES

1. For comparison of the two rankings, see Appendix, Table 3.

2. The only difference between the two is the absence of ties, in the case of respondents ranking all 30 occupations, between *enlisted man in the armed forces* and *owner of a sari-sari store*, on the one hand, and *barber* and *bus driver*, on the other hand.

3. Spearman's *rho* given by the formula $R = 1 - 6\Sigma d^2/n^3\text{-}n$ where n is the number of items ranked and d is the ranks assigned to a given item.

4. Cf. Chapter III, p. 82, for the designation of each Roman numeral group.

5. It was necessary to limit the number of categories in order to have sufficient cases in each group to make the analysis meaningful.

6. Of course, this may be due to the fact that instead of *manager of a business company* we gave to rural respondents as stimulus *manager of a rice mill*, with whom they would be more familiar. But it is possible that this occupation in the rural areas is not a "neutral" one as far as the feelings of our respondents, many of whom are engaged in farming and consequently may feel exploited by such a person as far as price received for their rice.

CHAPTER VI

CONCLUSION

SUMMARY OF THE DATA

In wending our way through numerous facets of the Filipino occupational structure, some definite patterns emerge as guideposts. The major intergenerational changes in our urban sample were:

1) the increase of clerical and sales persons,
2) the increase in the proportion of semi-skilled workers, and
3) the decline of persons engaged in farming.

This seems to reflect an increasing degree of urbanization and industrialization, at least in the community near Manila which we studied. Another marked feature is the high degree of satisfaction which both blue-collar and white-collar workers feel with their present occupation. Comparing themselves to their fathers in respect to education and socio-economic status (at comparable stages in their lifetime), our respondents feel much less worse off; older, white-collar workers felt substantially better off in comparison to their fathers than did younger, blue-collar workers. As far as general occupational preference, white-collar jobs are much more desirable to white-collar workers than to blue-collar workers; even so, blue-collar workers are pretty evenly divided as to which of these two sorts of employment they prefer. Of desired types of occupations, white-collar workers have a clear preference for the professions; blue-collar workers give a slight preference to skilled occupations first and clerical and sales employment second. If we consider what occupations respondents would advise their children to enter, the professions are selected by white-collar *and* blue-collar workers much more than any other occupational category. Of the reasons given for selecting an occupation for their children, the *economic factor* (wages, standard of living, economic security) was more frequently mentioned than any other single factor; one-fourth of white-collar workers and two-fifths of blue-collar workers stressed this reason. The second most frequently given reason was *service* to the country or to the community (or to mankind); one can say that this represents a "collectivity-orientation" which neatly complements the economic "self-orientation." If one considers the reasons given for the occupation which the respondent would *personally like to have*, the economic factor is again most prominent, but not as much as for the children's occupations; for both blue-collar and white-collar workers, *service to the country* (etc.) is no longer the second most cited factor--*intrinsic work satisfaction* and working conditions are mentioned more often.   Finally, of the reasons given by respondents as to what they like best about their *present* occupation, *intrinsic work satisfaction* is given ahead of *working conditions* or *economic* consideration having the next highest frequency. It may be remembered that these two were also the most frequently cited reasons for advising children to enter a particular occupation, although the order was reversed. For placing occupations at the bottom of the rank order, the *economic* frame of reference was stressed above the *degradation* involved in the work. It is interesting to note that low wages or insufficient pay was also the reason cited most often as the most unsatisfactory aspect of the present occupation of respondents.   Hardly any respondents mentioned *degradation* as the thing they most disliked about their occupation (*working conditions* was mentioned second), but one must realize that admitting that one's occupation is ignoble would somehow be very disturbing to the ego.

There is a notable continuity between what the individual desires as an occupation for his children, on the one hand, and his prestige evaluation of occupational roles, on the other. Just as the professions and semi-professions are desired for children more than any other occupational category, so are they given a higher social prestige rating than any other group. In a similar fashion, semi-skilled and especially unskilled work, which are least desired by respondents for their children, are the lowest rated occupational groups.

Of the various indices used in differentiating our sample in the ranking of occupations, *locality, religion,* and *language* proved to be somewhat more discriminating than *education, age, sex, income,* or *nature of the work* (as we have used that term); but it must be remembered that this is very relative since on any single variable the overall agreement was very high. One might argue that locality, religion, and language are perhaps more fundamental expressions of cultural differences, that they are more basic in molding different *Weltanschauungen*, than are the other factors we used; since our differences are relatively small, we must admit this is a tentative conclusion.

COMPARISON TO OTHER COUNTRIES[1]

To correlate the evaluation of occupations in the Philippines which seemed most similar or identical to those in other countries. The countries chosen were the United States (the NORC study), Great Britain, New Zealand, Japan, and Germany.[2] The Japanese and German data were taken from the article of Rossi and Inkeles; data for the other nations were obtained from the original sources. Below is shown the number of similar or identical occupations rated between the Philippines and these countries:[3]

	U.S.	Great Britain	New Zealand	Japan	Germany
Philippines	18	18	10	10	31

| total number of occupations in reported study | 88 | 30 | 30 | 30 | 38 |

Since our study had used *ranks*, and the other studies (with the exception of Germany) had used *scores*, the latter were converted into ranks, in order to make direct comparisons possible. Rank correlation coefficients (rhos) were computed for comparable occupations with the following results:

	U.S.	Britain	Great New Zealand	Japan	Germany
Philippines	.96	.96	.96	.93	.88

The average correlation was .94, which indicates a marked agreement between the Philippines and other countries. This high agreement is all the more interesting since the Philippines is essentially a non-industrial nation. Even if we compare separately our rural and our urban samples with such an industrialized society as the United States, we find the correlation coefficients to be, respectively .93 and .955. These factors suggest that it is not the industrial order *per se* which gives stability to the prestige hierarchy of occupations on a cross-national basis.[4]

For comparable occupations, *physician* ranks first in the Philippines as is also the case in the United States, Great Britain, New Zealand, and Russia. Our respondents also placed four other professions (*lawyer, engineer, university professor*, and *priest*, in that order) ahead of *business manager*, which is similar to the pattern in the United States; in other countries, *business manager* or its equivalent tends to have a higher rating vis-à-vis the professions. Just as in the Philippines, the prestige hierarchy of occupations in other countries elevates *officer in the armed forces* above *school teacher*. Following these professional or government occupations, *farmer* is usually ranked next in all countries, including the Philippines. Clerical and sales occupations also show a relatively uniform standing, being placed in the middle of status ratings in the Philippines as well as other nations. *Carpenter*, as representative of skilled occupations, is placed in the Philippines higher than semi-skilled or unskilled occupations (such as *factory worker, construction worker, road repairman*), and this pattern is also found in industrialized societies. In the Philippines, *barber* and *bus driver* are given about the same rating near the bottom of the hierarchy as in the United States and Japan. Finally, unskilled menial labor (*road repairman* in the Philippines, *street sweeper* and *garbage collector* in the United States) has either the lowest or one of the lowest standings in all the reported studies. In the Philippines the very bottom of the prestige hierarchy is given to *domestic servant* for a multiplicity of reasons: very low wages, lack of mobility, low requirements needed, degradation of work, etc.[5]

From this brief comparison, it appears that the Philippines, although primarily an agricultural-underdeveloped area, shares the same pattern of occupational evaluation as urban-industrial nations. To reiterate, the pattern is briefly as follows: with the exception of a few highly placed government posts (which are atypical of other occupations in respect to the duration of incumbency), the professional group is given the highest overall prestige rating, followed by the managerial and executive group of the industrial system; clerical, sales, and skilled occupations are more or less in the middle of the prestige hierarchy, with semi-skilled and unskilled occupations, in that order, at the bottom.

The consistency of this pattern in various cross-national studies, reinforced by our data on a country fairly unlike previously reported ones, gives weight to a '"structuralist" position suggested by Rossi and Inkeles. But, as we shall make clear in the next and final section, we wish to adopt a "structural" viewpoint different form the one of these authors. Their model suggests that it is the spread and introduction of the industrial order, described as "highly coherent system, relatively impervious to marked influence arising out of traditional culture patterns," which is responsible for occupations having roughly the same standing relative to each other regardless of their national cultural setting. Our argument is that if this were the case, then one should find only one set of norms, only one fundamental "definition of the situation" in relation to which occupations are evaluated. if the paramount frame of reference were to be given by the industrial order, then why is it that occupations emanating from this particular sub-system of the occupational structure are ranked *below* the professions and government posts? Why is it that our data, along with some of the other studies, indicate that there is a plurality of frames of reference which seem to be independent of one another?

Also, there is the fact that respondents in the Philippines, an underdeveloped country, are in essential agreement with respondents in urban-industrial societies as to the relative prestige rating of comparable occupations; using the Philippines as a "control," it seems dubious that it is the industrial order alone which accounts for cross-national consensus. Furthermore, it seems questionable to treat the industrial order as a monolithic structure or a "highly coherent system." For example, what is the relationship between a factory system oriented to the production of technological goods and a bureaucratic firm oriented to the production of services, and how is this relationship reflected in the prestige hierarchy of occupations within the industrial order differs markedly from the prestige hierarchy of pre-industrial economic organizations such as the medieval guild system? In other words, does not this "structuralist" position fall into the fallacy of misplaced concreteness by identifying a part with the whole?

If these contentions are valid, then a new approach must be sought to unify the research into occupational stratification on a cross-national basis.

CONCLUDING POSTSCRIPT:
TOWARD A THEORY OF OCCUPATIONAL STRATIFICATION

It appears to the writer that there are two general methods available in analyzing occupational stratification, or the prestige evaluation of occupational roles. The first is the historical method. Following this particular procedure one would study the historical development of an occupational role in its various manifestations within a particular socio-cultural system. the prestige standing of a particular occupation would be explained in terms of a historical setting. For example, the high status of *priest* in the Philippines would be understood in terms of the enormous influence of the Catholic Church in secular and spiritual matters, an influence which it has exercised ever since the arrival of Spanish conquistadores four centuries ago. The occupations of *physician* and *lawyer* were highly evaluated by the Spanish value-system, and this attitude was reinforced during the American administration, so that it is a natural historical consequence that these occupations rank very high today.

We could continue in this vein for every occupation on our list, but we are confronted with at least three serious obstacles in carrying out such an historical approach. The first is that not only is this a very laborious method, but also that historical materials concerning the relative standing of prestige occupations are very scant, difficult to obtain, and at best limited to a few occupations. The second limitation is that the historical method is on the whole inadequate to understand the prestige standing of relatively new roles in the occupational structure, such as *factory worker, office clerk, manager of a business company*, etc. At best we would be forced to seek prototypes of these roles in the previous occupational structure and to interpolate prestige standings, which might not always be facile or valid. The third objection to the historical method is that by its very nature it makes cross-national comparisons quite difficult, if not altogether impossible; one would tend to be impressed with the uniqueness of the socio-cultural setting of a given occupation and the various historical factors that have given rise to its prestige standing.

If these barriers are no mere chimeras but rather serious impediments, then perhaps a more suitable method is an analytical-structural approach which does allow meaningful cross-national comparisons. The writer would like to suggest that what has come to be called the "General Theory of Action" by Parsons and his associates[6] is particularly useful in providing the tools for such an approach. According to this framework, every social system is faced with four fundamental functional problems, which are analytically distinct aspects of the system in question. Every social system has as one of its problems that of "goal-orientation"--of deciding what are the desirable aims for the collectivity and what policy decisions must be made to reach these goals. Another problem is that of "adaptation" to the environment, which may be considered as the manipulation of situational objects requisite for the achievement of the goals of the members comprising the collectivity. In order that the members of the social system show at least some amount of cohesion and solidarity in their role performance, the internal problem of "integration" must perforce be coped with; if there is no minimal solution to this aspect, the specter of Hobbes' *bellum ominum contra omnes* will loom large and threatening. The fourth aspect of any social system we interpret to be that of common values, which are instrumental in relating the various parts of the system to one another and in motivating the societal members to participate in the system; in a sense, this area constitutes the ethos of a particular social system.

This scheme, presented here in skeletal form only, has the great advantage of being applicable to every type of social systems, including, of course, societies. We can then go on to say that every society that has any extensive division of labor will have occupational roles which can analytically be located in one of the four functional areas we have discussed. Every society will have an occupational role concerned with imparting to the societal members the basic values and cultural traditions of the system, such as the *priest* or the *educator*.[7] Likewise, every society will have occupational roles designed to make policy decisions for members of the collectivity in respect to both internal matters and external affairs with other collectivities; these occupations dealing with "problems of state" may take such varied forms as President of the United States, paramount chief, elders of a council, monarch, etc., but their functional significance is essentially the same, regardless of the cultural setting. Other occupational roles will tend to focus in the "adaptive" area (such as farmer, carpenter, factory worker, basket weaver, poultry raiser, etc.); they will be concerned with providing the commodities necessary to societal members. Lastly, certain occupational roles will be found which help to regulate individuals to other individuals and to the normative order of the system; these occupations might be lawyer, judge, policeman, and even physician.[8]

Because each of these four areas has a different functional significance for a society, we postulate that, analytically at least, there will be four fundamentally different prestige hierarchies in the occupational structure. We also acknowledge that at a particular time the solution of the problems of one particular area may be considered more essential or critical than those of other areas, and that consequently the prestige evaluation of at least some occupations in this sector may have relatively greater standing than those of other areas; for example, in war time the prestige of the military may become greater than that of, say, educators. But since these four separate sectors are inherent in any social system,m we categorically deny that the prestige rating of the occupational structure will *always* be subsumed under the *same* subdivision of the system. The solution of the problems of each structure is never fixed and permanent; every aspect is susceptible to changing conditions, and no empirical social system has ever been completely immune to change. Since every period will be forced to solve problems in all areas, some occupations in each of the four basic sectors will have a functional significance for the survival of the members of the system; therefore, each substructure of the social system in question will have its own prestige hierarchy, which is irreducible and cannot be derived from that of another dimension. The prestige accruing to occupations whose function is to regulate the coordination of societal members is of a different order from that belonging to occupations which lie in the adaptive area, and so on. On the other hand, this does not mean that the general prestige standing of a group of occupations in one sector of society will not be greater or less than that of other sectors for a given period. Certain functional problems will loom larger in one situation than do other problems and the solving of these imperatives will increase the prestige of certain occupations suited for this task.

The use of historical material would be very strategic in seeking to establish whether in the development of particular countries there tends to be a regular pattern in the relative emphasis of each sector--for example, if there tends to be the sequence of first establishing common values (general orientation to the world), then stressing the regulation and coordination of members (the problem of order), then greater emphasis on adapting and adjusting to the external environment and developing a differentiated economy. Finally, in this evolutionary scheme one might find that the increase in the size and population of the collectivity together with increasing contact with other collectivities and to place a greater emphasis on deciding common goals and carrying out such policy decisions. Undoubtedly, different societies, due to their particular socio-cultural setting, may have different patterns of development; but the forms of the patterns--if our analysis is correct--are theoretically limited to 24 different ones.[9] It may also be, of course, that there is no such serialization and that only randomness prevails; only actual historical data of a cross-national sort will answer this question.

If our framework is logical and empirically substantiated, then several implications can be seen arising from this model. First, to treat the professions, for example, as a somehow organically related group is erroneous; the functional significance of a particular professional role is different from that of another, although naturally more than one profession may be located within the same area of the social system. The fact that the professions as a group are given a very high prestige standing does not mean that it is because they are professions *per se* that they are highly regarded as a group;

rather, it is because they are individually at the top of various prestige hierarchies in different areas, due to their functional significance in different aspects of society. *Physician* and *lawyer* contribute to solving fundamental integrative problems which are ever-present in almost all societies which have any concern over the health of their members, on the one hand, and the disposition of property and orientation of members to some sort of a normative order (the problem of deviance), on the other. Therefore, we should expect that these occupations or their analogous roles, will consistently have a high prestige standing; likewise, as long as the relation between the members of a social system and some non-empirical, transcendental order is considered as embodying basic societal values, the role of the *priest* or its functional equivalent (Shaman, witch doctor, minister) will always be considered prestigeful.

Engineer, architect, and *scientist* (e.g., *chemist, physicist*, etc.) are examples of professions of crucial importance in the "adaptive" sector of the occupational structure; they are essentially concerned with technological mastery of situational conditions. Since their work is necessary for securing the material welfare of individuals and in some cases that of the collectivity, it is not too surprising to find their prestige rating high. Other factors contributing to their high status are their relatively high pay, their length of training, and a usually stable and secure occupational career.

Of course, not only will the same function be performed by different occupational roles in contrasting societies, but one should also expect the possibility that in the historical development of a particular socio-cultural system, different occupations have performed the same function. However, this does not bar us from making meaningful comparisons. In any event, since the professions by and large contribute to the solving of basic functional problems in different sectors of society, they stand to have as a whole a relatively quite high prestige standing. But, as we have suggested, this does not imply that they are all somehow "organically" related, at least not in the functional terms we have been using.

We can say, tentatively, that the prestige standing of an occupation is largely given by the particular dimension of the social system wherein it is chiefly located. This standing is also to some extent attributable to the given occupation's participation in the other sectors of the society, and to its ability to command the resources and embody the facilities of spheres other than its own. To the extent that an occupation is able to enjoy as much as possible the facilities and rewards of as many aspects of the social system as possible, its prestige will rank very high in comparison to an occupation which cannot do this. Such an occupation which has diversified the basis of its popularity or social prestige will be in a very good position to weather changes in the structure of the social system.

The consistently very high prestige of medical professions in almost all industrial societies is, by this analysis, definitely not an anachronism but the reflection of a social reality. First, health is every problematical and the occupation(s) which are concerned with maintaining the health of persons are bound to be highly regarded in industrial and non-industrial societies. Second, medical professions in industrial societies have a relatively favorable economic position; their earning power is higher than the average for all occupations. Finally, regardless of individual motivations, the institutionalized definition of the medical practitioner tends to focus on service to others, rather than personal gain. This coupled with the possession of knowledge and skills arrived at by a rather long training process (which know-how is not easily accessible to the majority of individuals) and a long tradition of respect and dignity are factors in giving this occupation a high standing in the value-area of a society. These various components are advantageous enough to preserve the stability of the high prestige rating of the physician. On the other hand, the priestly profession tends to lost its overall prestige once the process of secularization develops. Its knowledge of the mysterious, its communication with the transcendental tend to be relegated to a secondary rank; the knowledge of the scientist concerning the empirically mysterious tends to have a greater functional significance for society than that of the priest.[10] The economic position of the minister tends to become more unfavorable in relation to other occupations, since the acquisition of wealth as a motivational factor in a "sacred" occupation is usually frowned upon. Our data indicate that service to the collectivity and economic position are the most important frames of reference (at least judging by how often these are mentioned) in evaluating the social prestige of occupations; therefore, one should not be too surprised to find a decline in the prestige evaluation of the clergy or its equivalent.

High government officials continue to have a very favorable prestige standing, on par with the professions, for several reasons. In a sense, they are "collective representations" of the normative order and of the collectivity itself. Their decisions affect the welfare of the whole society, in both internal and external affairs; in formulating policies for the collectivity they exercise great power over individual actions. Their economic position is also quite favorable in comparison to the rest of the occupational structure. These, and other factors, contribute to the high standing of these occupations.

On the other hand, unskilled occupations as a group tend to have a low prestige rating for a plurality of factors. Most of these occupations are considered as degrading menial labor; chances for improvement are slight; there is little or no autonomy; training and talents are minimal; working conditions are on the whole strenuous; employment tends to be seasonal; financial remunerations for the work performed are lower than for other types of occupations. Unskilled occupations can be said to have a low standing within the "adaptive" area wherein they are chiefly located; they tend to be cut off form other sectors and have little influence on the actions of societal members, who have few, if any, contacts with persons in these occupations. It would be very interesting to find out why, psychologically, these occupations are considered "distasteful," if not actually "degrading." Sociologically, one might argue that their status is a reflection of their lack of functional importance but this does not explain the psychological opprobrium attached to such occupations as *ditch digger, garbage collector*, and *road worker*.

This sort of analysis of the prestige of occupations could be pursued in other sectors of the occupational structure (such as commercial, skilled, and unskilled work), but unfortunately this would take us too far beyond the scope of the present study which is intended to be suggestive rather than exhaustive.

To give a last *coup d'oeil* at what we have done, we have sought to show some of the salient aspects of the occupational structure of an underdeveloped area, how the prestige grading of occupations in the Philippines resembles that of other societies, and finally what general theoretical considerations can be made. It is hoped that in suggesting what are some of the avenues of research offered by the theoretical framework we have advanced, we have been able to plant a few signposts in the way of future studies on occupational stratification.

labor omnia vincit

NOTES

1. For purposes of economy and simplicity, we shall limit ourselves to the countries mentioned by Rossi and Inkeles in their article.

2. The Soviet Union is left out because there were too few comparable occupations.

3. See Appendix, Table 6, for the specific occupations in each of the other nations which could be compared to the Philippines.

4. The only alternative explanation as to why respondents in the Philippines show such a high agreement with persons in the United States would be that the American administration in the Philippines imparted to a very great extent the values of the American occupational structure; such an assertion is hard to prove or disprove given the lack of historical documentation regarding the prestige hierarchy of occupations during the Spanish regime.

5. Although many respondents indicated that the reason for the low status of this occupation was that it was a remnant of Spanish colonization, that domestic servants are vestiges of slavery, the writer was informed that persons in that occupation do make a prestige differentiation within their occupational group. Domestic servants who work for foreigners, especially Americans, are deemed to have more prestige than those who work for Filipinos, presumably because of the better (one is tempted to say more egalitarian) treatment and more substantial wages received in working for the former.

6. Of the now voluminous writings devoted to this theoretical scheme, perhaps the most concise summary is to be found in Talcott Parsons, "Some Comments on the State of the General Theory of Action," *American Sociological Review*, XVIII (Dec. 1953): 618-31.

7. It must be kept in mind that a particular individual, especially in a society characterized by a relatively low degree of social differentiation, may have more than one occupation. It is also imperative to note that the same occupation may have more than one functional role; great care must be observed in remembering

114 *The Evaluation of Occupations*

the perspective or point of reference form which one views a particular occupation.

8. We place the physician, or its equivalent, in this area because a fundamental prerequisite to interacting or relating to other members is a certain minimum of health. From this aspect, the role of the physician is an integrative one.

9. Since there are four dimensions, the total number of possible patterns of development is 4 ! = 24.

10. But the priest tends to remain important for individuals in *rites de passage* such as birth, marriage, and death. As long as individuals recognize the existence of a transcendental order to which they feel related and which cannot be manipulated by rational, scientific methods, the office of the priesthood will have functional significance.

APPENDIX

TABLE 1. Level of Job Satisfaction by Age, White-Collar and Blue-Collar Workers

VS	S	I	D	VD	DK	NA	N
White-collar workers							
Under 40 years of age:							
45	106	1	13	1	1	3	170
%26	62	*	8	*	*	2	98
Over 40 years of age:							
45	90	2	8	3	1	7	156
%20	58	1	5	2	*	5	100
TOTAL							
90	196	3	21	4	2	10	326
Blue-collar workers							
Under 40 years of age:							
15	116	2	31	4	3	9	180
% 8	65	1	17	2	2	5	100
Over 40 years of age:							
16	77	0	18	2	1	9	128
%12	60	0	18	2	1	7	100
TOTAL:							
31	193	2	54	6	4	18	308
%10	63	1	17	2	1	6	100

VS-very satisfied S-satisfied I-indifferent VD-very dissatisfied
DK-don't know NA-not applicable N-number

TABLE 2. Level of Job Satisfaction, by Occupational Groups

Group	VS	S	I	D	VD	DK	NA	N
I	34	75	--	7	1	1	2	120
	28%	62%		6%	1%	1%	2%	
II	18	19	--	2	--	--	--	39
	46%	49%		5%				
III	5	12	1	1	1	--	2	22
	23%	5 4 . 5 %	4.5%	4.5%	4.5%		9%	
IV	12	31	1	4	1	1	1	51
	23%	61%	2%	8%	2%	2%	2%	
V	21	59	1	7	1	--	5	94
	22%	63%	1%	8%	1%		5%	
VI	10	49	1	8	1	2	3	74
	14%	60%	1%	11%	1%	3%	4%	
VII	4	70	1	20	2	1	7	111
	4%	68%	1%	18%	2%	1%	6%	
VIII	1	23	--	11	3	1	3	42
	2%	55%		26%	7%	2%	7%	
IX	13	21	--	3	--	--	4	41
	32%	51%		7%			10%	
X	3	24	--	11	--	--	1	39
	8%	61%		28%			3%	
TOTAL	121	389	5	74	10	6	28	633

TABLE 3. Ranking of Occupations

Occupation	Respondents ranking 11-29 occupations	Respondents ranking all 39 occupations
barber	26	25
bus, jeepney driver	25	26
carpenter	22	20
congressman	5	2
construction worker	21	22
domestic servant	30	30
engineer	4	4
enlisted man	14	15
factory worker	23	23
farm tenant	20	21
farmer	10	11
fisherman	19	19
gas station attendant	27	27
int. school teacher	9	9
lawyer	3	3
mgr. business co.	7	7
midwife	17	12
office clerk	15	13
officer (military)	8	8
owner, sari-sari store	13	13
physician	1	1
policeman	12	14
priest	2	6
produce peddler	29	29
professional artist	11	10
road repairman	28	28
salesman	18	17
sugar plant. worker	24	24
tailor	16	18
university professor	6	5

$$R \text{ (rho)} = +.98$$

TABLE 4

Ranking of Occupations by Individual Occupational Group

Occupation	Occupational Group*									
	I	II	III	IV	V	VI	VII	VIII	IX	X
barber	25	25	27	25	23	25	26	29	25	26
bus, jeepney driver	26	29	21	25	26	26	25	24	22	25
carpenter	20	19	22	21	20	20	22	18	18	20
congressman	2	7	3	3	2	2	4	1	1	1
construction worker	22	23	23	24	21	18	21	20	20	23
domestic servant	30	30	30	30	30	30	30	30	30	30
engineer	4	3	4	3	3	3	3	3	6	5
enlisted man	10	17	13	16	17	16	15	11	12	15
factory worker	24	19	20	22	22	23	20	21	20	21
farm tenant	21	18	15	18	24	22	23	25	17	22
farmer	11	10	10	12	13	11	13	16	14	12
fisherman	19	21	23	18	19	21	19	22	26	18
gas. st. attendant	28	26	26	27	28	27	27	26	23	28
int. school teacher	9	8	7	9	9	9	9	9	8	10
lawyer	5	3	2	2	4	4	2	2	3	3
mgr. business co.	7	3	9	5	6	6	7	7	11	7
midwife	12	12	13	11	12	14	14	15	9	13
office clerk	13	15	16	14	11	12	12	10	14	14
officer (armed forces)	8	8	7	7	8	6	6	5	7	6
owner sari-sari	15	14	16	17	16	15	16	14	16	16
physician	1	1	1	1	1	1	1	4	2	2
policeman	14	13	12	14	14	13	11	13	10	11
priest	6	3	6	8	7	8	7	8	4	8
produce peddler	29	27	29	28	28	29	29	27	29	27
professional artist	10	10	11	10	10	10	10	12	12	9
road repairman	27	27	28	28	27	28	28	28	28	29
salesman	17	16	18	14	15	17	17	17	24	17
sugar plant. worker	23	24	25	23	25	24	24	23	27	24
tailor	18	22	19	20	18	19	18	19	19	19
university professor	3	2	5	6	5	5	5	6	5	4

*See page 58 for the designation of each occupational group.

TABLE 5. Standard Deviation of Occupations from Their Mean Rank by Age of Respondents

Under 40 years old		40 years old and over	
occupation	**s.d.**	**occupation**	**s.d.**
physician	3.88	physician	4.02
engineer	4.22	university professor	4.14
domestic servant	4.38	school teacher	4.38
school teacher	4.59	engineer	4.39
barber	4.68	barber	4.75
tailor	4.78	road repairman	4.84
gas station attendant	4.88	tailor	4.88
produce peddler	4.93	gas station attendant	4.93
university professor	5.12	carpenter	4.96
policeman	5.24	produce peddler	4.98
carpenter	5.25	midwife	5.03
salesman	5.35	factory worker	5.15
bus, jeepney driver	5.36	domestic servant	5.24
factory worker	5.44	bus driver	5.27
sugar plant. worker	5.49	office clerk	5.39
road repairman	5.50	lawyer	5.41
officer (military)	5.50	construction worker	5.54
office clerk	5.53	officer (military)	5.56
mgr. business co.	5.61	owner, sari-sari store	5.72
owner, sari-sari store	5.67	mgr. business co.	5.73
lawyer	5.71	policeman	5.81
fisherman	5.88	priest	5.85
midwife	5.92	sugar plant. worker	5.95
construction worker	6.15	fisherman	5.96
professional artist	6.33	congressman	6.04
priest	6.44	enlisted man	6.14
farm tenant	6.46	farm tenant	6.20
congressman	6.56	professional artist	6.46
enlisted man	6.57	salesman	6.72
farmer	7.45	farmer	7.13

TABLE 6.   Occupations in Other Countries Comparable to Those Used in the Philippine Study (arranged in their respective rank order)

United States	**Great Britain**	small indep. farmer
physician	medical officer	tailor
college professor	country solicitor	carpenter
Representative in Congress	business manager	barber
minister	non-conformist minister	bus driver
lawyer	farmer	fisherman
civil engineer	elementary school teacher	road worker
professional artist	policeman	*tied
captain in regular army	routine clerk	**Germany**
pub. school teacher	carpenter	university professor
farm owner and operator	agri. labourer (sugar plant. worker)**	doctor
tenant farmer		minister
policeman	**New Zealand**	major in armed forces
carpenter	same occupations as Great Britain	electrical engineer
corporal in regular army		elementary school teacher
machine operator in factory	**Japan**	farmer
barber	doctor	tailor
streetcar motorman (bus or jeepney driver)**	university professor	barber
gas station attendant	elementary school teacher	carpenter
	Buddhist priest	machine operator (factory worker)**
	retail store owner	non-commissioned officer
	company office clerk	street peddler
	policeman*	

(**in certain cases the equivalent occupation used in the Philippines study is placed in parentheses)

BIBLIOGRAPHY

SELECTED WORKS ON
OCCUPATIONAL STRATIFICATION

Bogardus, Emory S., "Occupational Distance," *Sociology and Social Research*, XII (1927): 73-79.

Campbell, John D., "Subjective Aspects of Social Status" (Ph.D. thesis, Harvard University, 1952).

Centers, Richard, "Attitude and Belief in Relation to Occupational Stratification," *Journal of Social Psychology*, XXVII (1948): 159-185.

Congalton, A.A., "The Social Grading of Occupations in New Zealand," *British Journal of Sociology*, IV (1953): 45-60.

Counts, George S., "The Social Status of Occupations," *School Review*, 1925.

Davies, A.F., "Prestige of Occupations," *British Journal of Sociology*, III (1952): 134-147.

Deeg, Maethel E., and Paterson, Donald G., "Changes in Social Status of Occupations," *Occupations*, XXV (1947): 205-208.

Durkheim, Emile, *De la division du travail social*, 2nd edition (Paris: Felix Alcan, 1902).

123

124 *The Evaluation of Occupations*

Edwards, Alba, U.S. Department of Commerce, Bureau of the Census, *A Social-Economic Grouping of the Gainful Workers of the United States* (Washington: Government Printing Office, 1938).
Hall, John, and Jones, D. Caradog, "The Social Grading of Occupations," *British Journal of Sociology*, I 1950): 31-55.
Hatt, Paul K., "Occupation and Social Stratification," *American Journal of Sociology*, LV (1950): 533-542.
Japan Sociological Society, *Report of a Sample Survey of Social Stratification and Mobility in the Six Large Cities of Japan* (Tokyo, 1952).
Lastrucci, Carlo L., "The Status and Significance of Occupational Research," *American Sociological Review*, XI (1946): 78-84.
MacRae, Donald G., "Social Stratification," *Current Sociology*, II (no. 1), 1953-54.
Montague, J.B. Jr., and Pustilnik, B., "Prestige Ranking of Occupations in an American City (Seattle) with Reference to Hall's and Jones' Study," *British Journal of Sociology*, V (1954): 154-160.
Moser, C.A., and Hall, J.R., "The Social Grading of Occupations," in D.V. Glass, ed., *Social Mobility in Britain* (London: Routledge & Kegan Paul, Ltd., 1954), 29-50.
National Opinion Research Center, "National Opinion on Occupations" (mimeo, University of Denver, 1947).
_____, "Jobs and Occupations: A Popular Evaluation," *Opinion News*, IX (1947): 3-13.
Parsons, Talcott, "The Problems of Hierarchical Prestige-Ordering of Occupational Roles" (Harvard University, memorandum).
Rossi, Peter, and Inkeles, Alex, "Cross National Comparisons of Occupational Ratings," *American Journal of Sociology*, LXI (1956): 329-339.
Smith, Mapheus, "An Empirical Scale of Prestige Status of Occupations," *American Sociological Review*, VIII (1943): 185-192.
Sorokin, Pitirim, *Social Mobility* (New York: Harper & Brothers, 1927), esp. Ch. 6, "Occupational Stratification," 99-130.
Taft, Ronald, "The Social Grading of Occupations in Australia," *British Journal of Sociology*, IV (1953) 181-88.
Tiryakian, Edward A., "Towards a Sociology of Occupations" (B.A. thesis, Princeton University, 1952).

SELECTED WORKS ON THE PHILIPPINES

Alip, Eufronio M., *Political and Cultural History of the Philippines* (Manila: Alip & Brion, Pub., Inc., 1949).
Benitez, Conrado, *History of the Philippines*, rev. ed. (Boston and Manila: Ginn and Company, 1954).
Blair, Emma H., and Robertson, James A., *The Philippine Islands, 1493-1898*, 55 vols. (Cleveland: Arthur H. Clark Co., 1903-09).
Castillo A.V., *Philippine Economics* (Manila, 1949).
Malcolm, George A., *First Malayan Republic, The Story of the Philippines* (Boston: The Christopher Publishing House, 1951).
Morga, Antonio de, *Sucesos de las Islas Filipinas*, W.E. Retana, ed. (Madrid: Libreria General de Victoriano Suarez, Editor, 1910).
Osias, Camilo, *The Filipino Way of Life* (Boston: Ginn and Company, 1940).
Philippine Council for United States Aid, Industrial Development Branch, *Industrial Philippines: A Cross Section* (Manila: 1953).
Reyes, Pedrito, Grau-Santamaria, M., Beyer, H. Otley, and Veyra, J.C. de., *Pictorial History of the Philippines* (Quezon City, P.I., 1953).
Rivera, Generoso F., and McMillan, Robert T., *The Rural Philippines* (Manila: Office of Information, U.S. Mutual Security Agency, 1952).
_____, *An Economic and Social Survey of Rural Households in Central Luzon* (Manila: U.S. Operations Mission to the Philippines, 1954).
Spencer, J.E., *Land and People in the Philippines* (Berkeley and Los Angeles: University of California Press, 1954).